Their Time Has Come

The Rutgers Series in Childhood Studies
The Rutgers Series in Childhood Studies is dedicated to increasing our understanding of children and childhoods, past and present, throughout the world. Children's voices and experiences are central. Authors come from a variety of fields, including anthropology, criminal justice, history, literature, psychology, religion, and sociology. The books in this series are intended for students, scholars, practitioners, and those who formulate policies that affect children's everyday lives and futures.

Edited by Myra Bluebond-Langner, Board of Governors Professor of Anthropology, Rutgers University, and True Colours Chair in Palliative Care for Children and Young People, University College London, Institute of Child Health

Advisory Board

Perri Klass, New York University
Jill Korbin, Case Western Reserve University
Bambi Schiefflin, New York University
Enid Schildkraut, American Museum of Natural History and Museum for
    African Art

Their Time Has Come

Youth with Disabilities Entering Adulthood

VALERIE LEITER

RUTGERS UNIVERSITY PRESS

NEW BRUNSWICK, NEW JERSEY, AND LONDON

LIBRARY OF CONGRESS CATALOGING-IN-PUBLICATION DATA

Leiter, Valerie, 1965–
    Their time has come : youth with disabilities entering adulthood /
Valerie Leiter.
        p. cm. — (Rutgers series in childhood studies)
        Includes bibliographical references and index.
        ISBN 978–0–8135–5247–7 (hardcover : alk. paper) — ISBN 978–0–8135–5248–4
(pbk. : alk. paper) — ISBN 978–0–8135–5330–6 (e-book)
        1. Youth with disabilities—Services for.   2. Young adults with disabilities—
Education.   3. Young adults with disabilities—Employment.   I. Title.
    HV1569.3.Y68L45   2012
    362.4—dc23

                                                                2011023342

A British Cataloging-in-Publication record for this book is available
from the British Library.

Visit our Web site: http://rutgerspress.rutgers.edu

Manufactured in the United States of America

For Amy Robison,
from a fan

CONTENTS

ACKNOWLEDGMENTS

My profound thanks to the youths, parents, and professionals who told me about their experiences, and for their suggestions about how the transition to adulthood might be improved. Their words bring this book to life. I am also deeply grateful to the William T. Grant Foundation Scholars program, which funded this work. They offered more than funding—their emphasis on individual development applies not just to youths, but also to the scholars whom they sponsor. Bob Granger, Ed Seidman, Vivian Tseng, Tom Weisner, Brian Wilcox, and Irene Williams provided support and encouragement at just the right moments over the past five years.

One of the biggest challenges in any research study is to find people who are willing to participate, and a number of organizations and individuals went out of their way to help me because they believed that transition was such an important topic. For taking the time to provide me with advice and assistance, I would like to thank staff at the Asperger's Association of New England, Boston Center for Independent Living, Boston Chinatown Neighborhood Center, Boston College Campus School, Cotting School, Easter Seals of Massachusetts, Enable Inc., Federation for Children with Special Needs, Landmark School, Mass Arc, Massachusetts Department of Developmental Services, Massachusetts Family Voices, Massachusetts Rehabilitation Commission, Multicultural Center for Independent Living, New England Academy, Partners for Youth with Disabilities, Seven Hills, Toward Independent Learning and Living, and Urban Pride. Several colleagues and friends encouraged and helped me on this project. Although none can be held accountable for what follows, I appreciate their efforts to help me improve it. Penny Hauser-Cram, Dennis Hogan, Emily Ozer, and Kevin Roy offered constructive feedback on various parts of the manuscript. Oakley Hoerth and Jenifer McKim took turns taking care of our girls in our working moms' cooperative, Claire Goodwin accompanied me on outings, and Betsy Anderson and Diane Hammer kept me company when I took the time to stop and smell the roses.

Three research assistants made important contributions to this work. Lexie Waugh, who conducted the youth interviews and helped me code all the youth and parent interview data, deserves special recognition for her hard work, fresh insights, great people skills, and good company on long drives all over Massachusetts. Sheila Rosselli contributed terrific ideas and her time coding the professional data, and Jen Byers helped with some of the legal work and bore a heavy literature load.

My family has been incredibly supportive throughout. John is always there, cheering me on, and Esther and Evelyn were patient with me when I had to spend time with other people's families many evenings instead of with them. Breakfasts with my father-in-law, Wally, were a lifeline, as were weekly check-ins with my mom, Elizabeth, and my mother-in-law, Celia.

Finally, my thanks to the staff at Rutgers University Press, who were so helpful throughout the final stages of writing this book. I'd like to thank Myra Bluebond-Langer and Marlie Wasserman for their early encouragement when the book was not yet a book, Marilyn Campbell and Peter Mickulas for their smooth handling of all the details, Bobbe Needham for her thoughtful and constructive copyediting, and Catie Colliton for her thorough indexing.

Their Time Has Come

1

A Crisis Situation?

The current generation of youths with disabilities who are coming of age in the United States is the first to benefit from a wide range of disability programs and policies, from birth to adulthood. In the past fifty years, multiple federal disability policies have been created with the goal of increasing opportunities for individuals with disabilities. These changes in disability policy have been profound, as two profiles of high school students illustrate.

Youth Profiles: Frankie and Kayla

Frankie: College Bound

An extroverted and articulate junior attending his local public high school, Frankie described himself as "a musical theater fanatic" who hoped to pursue his "dream in New York."[1] Frankie attended occasional productions in New York City with family, listened to recordings in his free time, and participated on- and offstage in community theater productions. His intense involvement in musical theater meant that he had a large number of friends and acquaintances who shared his passion. He kept up with these people in person and through Facebook. A consummate social networker, "very much a people person," Frankie had even made online contact with a director in New York City. He was working on getting his driver's license, with advice and training from the Massachusetts Rehabilitation Commission (MRC).

Frankie was born with a physical condition that limited his mobility, and he used a wheelchair to get around. He had a very close relationship with his mother, Celie, who was completely supportive of his goals and has worked hard to advocate for him inside and outside school. Celie was fortunate to have a good friend who had extensive knowledge about disability laws and resources. This friend had a son several years older than Frankie who also used a wheelchair. The friend's extra years of experience, plus her professional work in the disability field, made her an invaluable resource on a range of topics, including adapted driving and colleges that provided good access for students with physical disabilities. Frankie received some special education services through his school under the Individuals with Disabilities Education Act (IDEA). Both Frankie and Celie participated in special education meetings at Frankie's school and seemed satisfied with the services that Frankie was receiving. Celie was not certain that acting was the right fit for Frankie as a long-term career. She thought that "he should broaden his horizons, because there are a lot of starting musical theater performance majors waitering or waitressing to get by . . . so I think he needs to be a little more diverse and maybe go into production." But she supported his goals and saw herself as playing a key advocacy role and encouraging him to take risks.

At school and outside it, Frankie was focused on his goal: to pursue a career in theater. He had already completed several theater internships, one of which was paid, during the school year and over the past two summers. He loved "just being around theater and seeing the magic that happens when you fill a room with people and they just go crazy." He was preparing to attend college, where he planned to continue his theater work.

Frankie was taking college preparatory classes in his junior year at his local suburban high school, including two honors classes. Unfortunately, Frankie did not receive much assistance from his guidance counselor at school. Frankie was relying primarily on his mother to help guide him through the college search process, plus a counselor at the MRC who gave them some advice about colleges that have good accessibility. He and his mother had already started visiting colleges to look at the physical accessibility of schools he might want to attend. Section 504 of the Rehabilitation Act and the Americans with Disabilities Act make it illegal for colleges to discriminate against Frankie because of his disability and gave him the right to accommodations to make college accessible to him. However, some colleges were more physically accessible than others, and he was looking for a campus that would allow him to get around as independently as possible. The summer before his senior year, Frankie planned to do summer stock again in a regional theater and was gearing up for the college application process.

Kayla: Work after Turning Twenty-two

At twenty years of age, Kayla was focused on gaining life and work skills that would help her find a job after high school. Kayla was entitled to stay in special education in her public school district until her twenty-second birthday under state law, due to her intellectual disability. She wanted to make the most of that time. Living with her aunt and uncle in an urban area, Kayla was attending a technical high school where she was taking applied academic classes and culinary classes, plus working as an intern in several job placements in her community. She loved to cook and did it not simply as a job, but also "as an activity—I do it with my cousins." Initially, Kayla had been placed in regular academic classes in high school, including classes in Spanish and Chinese, and her aunt had to help her advocate for herself to get placed in a program that gave her more applied job skills. This advocacy work was complicated by the fact that Kayla was over the age of eighteen and was legally an adult. Her aunt and uncle did not have guardianship of her. Instead of seeking guardianship, her aunt Kelsey had decided that she should mentor Kayla into learning how to advocate for herself. Before Kayla's annual Individual Education Program (IEP) meetings with special education staff, Kelsey would help her put together a statement plus a list of questions that she wanted to have answered. Kayla explained: "I got a chance to talk and my aunt helped me with it—that's why it says shared decision making." Kayla's extensive participation in these meetings with special education staff was very unusual—only a handful of youths in the study were mentored into taking an active role in advocating for themselves during special education meetings with school staff.

Kayla was serious about school and explained that not all the kids at her school felt the same way. Some smoked and skipped school. She said that recently, police had brought drug-sniffing dogs into her school and found marijuana, and a student had been caught with a gun at school. In contrast, she explained, "I'm not out here skipping and being silly, I'm there trying to learn how to get a job and so forth. Because I'm already twenty and I only got two more years left." Kayla understood that her classes at school supported her goals. She was taking life skills, science, math, and English, and said that she really needed the math and English "for getting a job." The English class helped her with her reading, and the math class worked on her arithmetic skills. She liked the science class because, "well, science, you learn about your body, you learn about how animals do things, you know? So it's kind of cool." In the life skills class, Kayla had been working on personal finance. She said she had learned: "Don't go overboard—see how I'm doing, that is because I have a folder in my room. Have I done everything, what I bought for, what I paid for, you know?"

After high school Kayla's goal was "hopefully [to] have a job. Hopefully, that's my goal setting, that's what I want to do." Ideally, she wanted a job as a dietary aide. Her high school had placed her in two internship settings out in the community to help her explore her interests and get some experience, and had helped her learn how to take the bus to work. One placement was doing food preparation at a large supermarket nearby and the other was as a dietary aide. Kayla was hoping to get a job at a nearby hospital but had experienced some difficulty keeping up with the pace of the work there. "But it didn't work so well," she said, "because my shop teacher went in there and she wasn't seeing enough progress to even think about trying to get me to have the job there, you know?" She had a job coach at first through her school, but when the school pulled the job coach it was hard for her to finish her assigned work fast enough. This frustrated Kayla, who said: "You have to be fast, like the snap of a finger. And that was part of the problem, because I wasn't fast enough in the dish room. But [the job coach] knew that I was making good progress." She felt that she could do the work with more practice, explaining: "I want to do more. I know I'm capable of doing more things." Kayla had decided that if the school didn't sponsor her for an internship doing the kind of work she wanted to do, she would volunteer over the summer to get more experience, to help her attain her career goal of being a dietary aide.

Maximizing Potential

Frankie and Kayla have benefited from disability policies that have been created over the past four decades. Both had the right to attend public schools all the way through high school, thanks to the Individuals with Disabilities Education Act (IDEA). Frankie had received disability services through the Massachusetts Rehabilitation Commission, which helped him become more independent and supported his career goals. And Frankie's goal of attending college was made possible by Section 504 of the Rehabilitation Act and Americans with Disabilities Act. Frankie and his mother perceived college to be open to him as a result of these pieces of federal legislation. Kayla was taking classes and receiving special education services aimed at helping her live independently and work as a dietary aide after high school. She was able to stay in high school until she aged out of special education at twenty-two, and she and her aunt had used Kayla's rights under IDEA to establish access to services that would support her career goal. Kayla's school was providing her with applied academic classes, vocational training, and internships that allowed her to gain work experience and skills in support of her goals.

Fifty years ago, Frankie's and Kayla's stories would have been less hopeful. Schools routinely refused admission to children and youths with disabilities. Frankie would not have had the right to have wheelchair access to his local high school, and many public school systems simply refused to educate students with intellectual disabilities like Kayla's. Kayla's family would have had to choose between placing her in an institution and keeping her at home with no public services or supports. Much of Frankie's and Kayla's potential as individuals would have been stifled by negative attitudes toward people with disabilities. Over the past fifty years, parents of children with disabilities and adults with disabilities fought hard to improve the opportunities of individuals with disabilities.

Contemporary disability policy in the United States attempts to improve the life trajectories of youths with disabilities by increasing the opportunities available to them across their entire lives. It does so by providing early intervention services to infants and toddlers with developmental disabilities and civil rights to public primary and secondary education, and by prohibiting discrimination in education and employment. Individuals' life courses are "embedded in and shaped by the historical times and places they experience over their lifetime" (Elder 1998, 3).[2] In Frankie's and Kayla's stories, we see two lives shaped by federal disability policies. Their success is not guaranteed—no one's is. But they have opportunities to strive for their goals and grow as individuals, and we can be hopeful that they will achieve their educational and employment aims.

Is There a Crisis?

How can we reconcile Frankie and Kayla's stories with a recent declaration by the National Council on Disability (NCD) and Social Security Administration (SSA) that there is "a crisis situation for youth with disabilities" in the United States? In their joint report on the status of youths with disabilities, the NCD and SSA cited four central problems: "poor graduation rates from high school, low employment rates after high school, low postsecondary participation, and an increasing number of youth receiving Social Security benefits and not leaving the rolls" (NCD 2000, 1). Is there a crisis? It is true that youths with disabilities as a group are still disadvantaged compared with their peers, but they have made significant strides to catch up over the past few decades. Many youths with disabilities transition to adulthood successfully according to traditional markers of adulthood, although others do not. These markers of adulthood are familiar to all of us—there is a series of steps laid out for all individuals approaching adulthood. They are expected to complete high school. These days, they are often expected to obtain some form of postsecondary education, either college or vocational training, so that they will be competitive in the labor force. They are supposed to get jobs. Eventually, they are expected to live on their own, separate from their parents. These traditional markers focus almost entirely on independence and self-sufficiency, reflecting broader social attitudes in the United States about who counts as a full adult.[3]

On each of these traditional markers of adulthood, youths with disabilities as a group lag a bit behind their peers. They are less likely to be employed for pay outside the home—57 percent, compared with 66 percent of seventeen- to twenty-one-year-olds in the general population (NCSER 2009). While 53 percent of youths in the general population went on to postsecondary education, 45 percent of those with disabilities did so. We need to acknowledge that disability shapes individuals' chances of attaining these traditional markers of adulthood and is therefore a fundamental cause of inequality in adulthood; we also need to recognize that the effects of disability vary depending upon its nature (Janus 2009).

Yet it is equally important to acknowledge that young people with disabilities are increasingly likely to attain these adult markers. They are more likely than in the past to complete high school and less likely to drop out of high school. In 2003, 70 percent completed high school, compared with just 54 percent in 1987—in fact, their high school completion rate is now comparable to that for all young people (Wagner et al. 2005). Youths with disabilities are also more likely than in the past to take college-preparatory classes (Wagner, Newman, and Cameto 2004).

But while statistical data allow us to track large-scale trends in the experiences of youths with disabilities as a group, they do not tell the whole story. They do not provide specific information about where youths and their parents see disability policies as helpful, and where and why they fall short. Young people's own stories are missing from our understanding of the transition to adulthood among youths with disabilities.

This book examines how federal disability policy trickles down to the lives of youths with disabilities who are coming of age, highlighting where it helps and where it does not. The next two stories help us understand where challenges and problems with disability policies remain, particularly problems with getting information and resources and uncertainty about work opportunities after high school.

Youth Profiles: Kaiser and Ricardo

Kaiser: Work First, Then Maybe Some College

When he was asked about what he likes to do in his free time, Kaiser replied: "Sports are my life." He liked "any sport I know how to play, basically," but admitted that baseball was his favorite. Kaiser also liked to play video games, including fighting games, role-playing games, and Guitar Hero. He was much less enthusiastic when talking about school. Kaiser was attending a private school that had a specialized program for students with Asperger syndrome. It was not until he was in second grade that he received testing for a disability, at his parents' request. His father, Bob, explained that "we could not get the district to accept that Kaiser had special needs. In second grade, we had testing done. And they said, 'Every-thing's fine.' And we knew it wasn't." Even after the testing, the school refused to acknowledge his condition, and it was not until the fourth grade that he was put on a Section 504 plan (which has fewer rights than an Individual Education Program [IEP] under IDEA). Finally, testing in the fifth grade resulted in a diagnosis on the autism spectrum. Kaiser's parents also filed a complaint with the state Department of Education, and eventually Kaiser got into his present school, after moving between several schools that did not attend to his needs fully. It had been a long road for Kaiser just getting to high school. His mother, Rose, explained that now they relied on the Asperger Association of New England for information and advice and had just started a parent support group at Kaiser's school.

Kaiser was looking forward to finishing school in two years. "Right now," he said, "I'm kind of sick of school." His parents understood his position, and while their initial vision was that Kaiser would attend college after high school, they were "scaling it down so that it may be [college] classes." Instead, they focused on helping him become "self-sufficient and gainfully employed." Kaiser explained: "When I am done with high school, I'd probably want to wait a year or two, then go to college. And I'm hoping to either be a photographer or a dog trainer." Asked how he became inter-ested in those jobs, he responded: "I don't know. My mom and dad say that I've always had a eye for pictures. So I guess that's what got me started in taking pictures. And I've always been interested in animals and loved animals, especially dogs. So it would really keep me busy and it would make me happy to be a dog trainer, or have a job with dogs." He had done agility training with his own dog and enjoyed it. Kaiser was not sure about colleges that might be a good fit and had not started searching for schools. "But if possible, I was hoping to find a school that had a really good photography class or was made specifically for animals," he said. His high school did not offer a photography class, but he spent some of his free time taking pictures.

In support of his goal to work after high school, Kaiser was participat-ing in a job readiness program at his high school, where he was learning "what you do in a job," such as, "like you want to be polite, do what your boss tells you without putting up a fuss. And what else should I say? Put your best effort into it." He wasn't sure what kind of job he might seek after high school. "I haven't really looked into it all that much, like what jobs are out there," he said. Kaiser's current life goals? "I'm hoping to get an apartment and get a job, then save up money and maybe buy a small house." Ideally, the house would have a large area around it where he could train dogs, and it would be in a suburban or rural area "that's peaceful and not too upbeat." Kaiser wanted to be near his parents, "so when they get older and unable to take care of themselves as well, I could drive up to them and help them out and stuff."

Ricardo: Day Program after Turning Twenty-two, Maybe

Ricardo, who was twenty years old, lived with his mother, father, and younger sisters in an apartment in an urban neighborhood. His parents immigrated to the United States before Ricardo and his sisters were born, and Ricardo was born in a large hospital in the city where he still lived. He loved to listen to music and to be with "other people like him, boys and girls," according to his mother, Maria. Ricardo was born with a condition that resulted in both physical and intellectual disabilities. These disabilities made it necessary for him to be pushed in a wheelchair for mobility and affected his communication. Ricardo did not speak but could choose between things that he wanted and used a basic communication board for some responses. He watched his mother intently, making eye contact when she talked to him.

Ricardo had received early intervention services after his birth, and had been in special education all the way through school. He attended a public school in the city where he lived, in a separate educational environment with other youths who had physical and intellectual disabilities. His mother was fairly happy with the services that the school provided, which included speech and language therapy, physical therapy, and occupational therapy, but was annoyed that the school provided his report cards and other materials in English only; she knew that she had the right to receive them in Spanish, her first language. Fortunately, she was able to read some English and thought herself fortunate compared with other Latino parents she knew whose children were also receiving special education services; those parents could not read any of the materials they received.

At the time, an occupational therapist was working with Ricardo on sorting objects, because Maria hoped that after high school Ricardo would be able to attend a day program that would include a sheltered work component. Maria was frustrated that she was unable to obtain any information from the Department of Developmental Services (DDS) about possible day program placements for Ricardo after he left high school, even though he was almost twenty-one and would transition from high school to adult services on his twenty-second birthday. Staff at DDS had helped Ricardo's parents apply for guardianship of him but were not working with them actively on transition issues. Maria was worried "because some parents tell me that maybe sometimes when the children leave [school], they don't have a place to work. So I think if he spent most of his life at school, he can miss it." Maria was emphatic that Ricardo would continue to live with them when he turned twenty-two, but she very much wanted him to be in a program where there was some kind of employment, where he would be with "other people like him" and would not be lonely during the day.

Maria was seeking information to help her advocate better for Ricardo and had recently turned to an urban Latino organization (City Life/Viva Urbana) and to the Federation for Children with Special Needs (a parent training and information center funded by the U.S. Department of Education) for information on transition. A few months before, she had found a day program she liked in a nearby town. She was at a local mall and noticed a staff person with some day program participants. "I saw someone going around the mall with them and I ask. [*Laughs.*] I asked. Yeah, because I say no one is doing nothing. I have to do something. I would like someone to say what choices I have in this."

Continuing Struggles

Compared with Frankie's and Kayla's families, Kaiser's and Ricardo's parents had to struggle more to get access to rights and services. Part of Kaiser's challenge stemmed from his school district's longstanding refusal to acknowledge his disability. Only when his parents complained to the state Department of Education did the school district budge, and when it did, Kaiser was placed in a private school outside the district. Kaiser's experiences in school were rocky; not surprisingly, he was simply looking forward to getting out of high school. Beyond that, his goals were fuzzier. Ricardo's mother was advocating for him but faced barriers to information and vague answers about possible services when Ricardo was an adult.

She was worried that Ricardo would end up at home full-time with no public services once his entitlement to special education ended on his twenty-
second birthday.

It would be folly to assume that disability policy has fixed all the
problems that youths with disabilities experience, as these two accounts
show. Not all young people know about and use their disability rights.
Not all parents and parental figures are savvy about the public resources
that exist. And disability policies cannot remove all constraints associated
with having a disability or change all individuals' attitudes about disability.
Youths with disabilities who are coming of age still face individual, structural, and attitudinal constraints in their lives. It is important for us to
understand where disability policies do and do not help at the ground
level, through their lived experiences.

This Study

Here, three sets of voices tell what it is like to come of age with a disability
in the United States today, and the role that disability policy plays in
promoting opportunities for them. Youths with disabilities provide the
primary voice, supplemented by the experiences of their parents and of
professionals who work with young people and parents on transition. Data
were collected in interviews of fifty-two youths with three kinds of disabilities and their parents (see the appendix)—nine had physical or sensory
conditions such as cerebral palsy, muscular dystrophy, blindness, or hearing impairment; seventeen had hidden disabilities (Asperger syndrome or
learning disabilities); and twenty-six had intellectual disabilities, including Down syndrome, autism, birthing and other injuries, and intellectual
disabilities of unknown origin.

The interviews give us insight into the hopes, dreams, experiences,
and resources that these young people bring to the transition from high
school. The wide range of disability types allows us to examine how disability policies affect lives and opportunities differently, depending upon
the nature of the youth's needs and the resources that are available to
address them. The young people's voices are highlighted whenever possible here. Parental perspectives are also incorporated throughout, as parents are still responsible for their children during their time in high school

and perform a tremendous amount of work on their behalf. The children are often not aware of all of the work that is being done for them behind the scenes, a dynamic not atypical for high school students in general. Often, youths and parents provided consistent accounts of transition planning. In instances in which youths' and parents' accounts diverge, those tensions are explored in some detail. The youth and parent perspectives are complemented by twenty interviews conducted with professionals in public agencies and community organizations that address disability and transition issues. These professionals confirmed that some of the issues that individual youths faced were pervasive (not merely anecdotal), highlighted innovative approaches to helping youths transition to adulthood, critiqued educational and service delivery systems, and provided recommendations for policy change.

The focus here is on disability. Other factors shape youths' opportunities in powerful ways, such as gender, race, ethnicity, socioeconomic status, and geographic location. These factors are incorporated here when they are relevant, which they often are. But this book focuses primarily on exploring the experiences of youths with very different kinds of disabilities to illuminate ways in which various disabilities and social resources may shape their experiences and opportunities. Young people with disabilities are often discussed as one homogeneous group in policy documents and in the public press, as though they all have similar experiences and expectations. Nothing could be further from the truth. These youths exit high school at different ages, headed for very different destinations. Their timing and destinations depend upon their aspirations and experiences, their abilities and disabilities.

The young people in this study were headed for one of three possibilities upon turning eighteen: remaining in special education for additional transition time past age eighteen, graduating from high school and attending college, or graduating from high school and seeking employment. Figure 1.1 shows these routes from high school into adulthood. All the youths with physical or sensory disabilities and the majority with hidden disabilities planned to graduate from high school, attend college, and work after they finished college. This was Frankie's planned route into adulthood. Kaiser was one of a handful of youths with hidden disabilities who planned to go out to work after high school; a few of this group thought

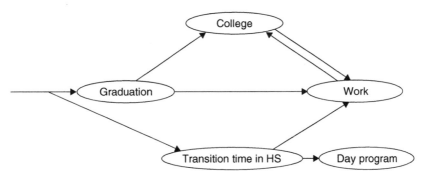

FIGURE 1.1. Routes from high school into adulthood planned by youth in this study.

they might go to college or vocational programs after working for a year or two. All but one of the youths with intellectual disabilities planned to spend additional transition time in high school until they turned twenty-two, when their entitlement to special education would end and their eligibility for state-funded adult services would begin. Those who stayed in special education until they turned twenty-two then planned to go to work or to adult day or residential programs after high school, depending upon their aspirations and abilities and their need for services. Kayla planned on working, and Ricardo's mother hoped to have him placed in a day program that would provide a sheltered workshop component. These three initial possibilities after high school—transition time, college, and work—were shaped by the youths' interests, by the skills and knowledge they had gained in high school, and by their disabilities.

2

The Rules Have Changed

One hundred years ago, a child born with a disability would have been kept at home and would have received no public services, or would have been placed in a public institution surrounded by others labeled as having similar disabilities. Such children became the responsibility of the state in which they resided and often had little or no contact with their families. Parents who chose to keep their children at home bore the entire responsibility for their education and care. There was no middle ground (see Leiter 2004b).

Physicians, social workers, and other professionals with whom parents came in contact tried hard to convince them to institutionalize their children young, even at birth. They told parents that they could not care for their children adequately at home and that the "state school" would give them the skills they needed. For example, in Washington State in the 1930s, some schools had public special education programs, but administrators used them to identify children to be sent to state institutions.[1] Schools did not want to serve children and youths with disabilities and largely were able to deflect parents' attempts to obtain public education for their children. By one estimate, only 15 percent of children with intellectual disabilities in the 1960s who were living with their families received special education in public schools (see Mackie 1969).

In a letter now housed at the Smithsonian Institution, a school staff member from the nurse's office at the Carlstadt, New Jersey, public schools wrote in 1951 to the New Jersey Parents Group for Retarded Children about a mother who demanded a public education for her children with intellectual disabilities, reporting that the mother refused to commit them to a state institution and "apparently has been unable to accept the fact that her children cannot be taught in the Public or Trade schools." The letter goes on to ask: "Do you have any literature, or suggestions which might aid us in helping this mother accept and solve her problem?"[2] Parents were on their own if they did not accept institutionalization as the public solution to caring for and educating their children.

Much has changed in the fifty years since. Now we have predominantly community-based education and services for children and youths with disabilities, as a result of incremental changes in federal law since the 1970s. Federal policies now give children and youths access to services to maximize their capabilities and civil rights legislation designed to remove architectural and attitudinal barriers. Infants and toddlers identified as developmentally disabled or delayed are eligible for early intervention services meant to maximize their development and provide support to their families. Children with disabilities have a right to a public education. And federal legislation has given children, youths, and adults with disabilities additional civil rights to improve their access to resources and to reduce discrimination against them.

Individuals with disabilities who are coming of age at this moment are the first generation in U.S. history to benefit throughout childhood from disability policies designed to improve opportunities for learning, working, and living in local communities. While earlier generations may have benefited from some of these changes, this is the first to have grown up entirely under these new rules. Yet many young people and their families are not entirely aware of these new rules and the rights they provide. This chapter asks and answers two questions: How and why were these new rules created? and How does disability policy now provide opportunities to youths with disabilities? The answer to the first summarizes the story of the disability rights movement as it relates to improving opportunities for youths with disabilities, helping us understand how and why we have the current rights and service systems. The answer to the second describes the resulting federal policies that currently provide rights and educational and employment services to youths with disabilities.

How Did We Get Here?

I bring a youth-focused lens to the story of the disability rights movement here, showing how it shaped the opportunities for young people with disabilities in the United States and helping us understand the origins of current policies and approaches. There were three waves of the disability rights movement. The first was organized by parents of children with disabilities, and the second by adults with physical disabilities. In the third wave, coalitions of parents, adults with a wide range of disabilities, and professionals who worked with people with disabilities collaborated to advocate for policy changes.

The Parents' Movement: Love and Homemade Bread

The institutionalization of children who were deaf or blind or had intellectual disabilities began in the 1800s and increased throughout the 1900s. As of 1970, 75 percent of institutions for people with intellectual disabilities had been built after 1950 (Trent 1994). At the same time, forces in U.S. society were starting to work against institutionalization. Beginning in the 1930s and 1940s, parents of children with disabilities, especially intellectual disabilities, began to organize through grassroots organizations, becoming one of the least recognized but most successful social movements in U.S. history. Parents who had been completely isolated reached out to other parents, often through newspaper ads. For example, in 1948, Anne Greenberg placed an ad in the *New York Post*: "To the mothers of retarded children: Are you interested in forming a cooperative nursery school for your children?" A similar ad had been placed in the *Bergen Evening Record* by a mother in New Jersey. In each case, the advertisement led to the establishment of a local group that developed a range of programs (Dybwad 1990, 27).

At first, parents' sights were set on smaller efforts, such as sending Christmas presents to children in institutions, forming play groups, and meeting other families whose children had the same diagnosis (see Dybwad 1983; Schwartzenberg 2005, 12).

Once organized, parents soon widened the scope of their goals, attempting to redefine their families as "normal" and seeking to reduce the stigma and social exclusion that they and their children experienced.

Celebrities such as Pearl Buck, Dale Evans, and Roy Rogers came forward to tell their stories of having children with intellectual disabilities. In 1962, Eunice Kennedy Shriver wrote about her family's experiences with her sister Rosemary in a *Saturday Evening Post* article: "Like diabetes, deafness, polio, or any other misfortune, mental retardation can happen in any family. It has happened in the families of the poor and rich, of governors, senators, Nobel prize winners, doctors, lawyers, writers, men of genius, presidents of corporations—the President of the United States" (Shriver 2004, 304).

The perception of family normalcy was not enough—parents wanted their children to have the same kinds of opportunities as other children. They wanted them to experience the typical childhood rites of passage, such as summer camps and swimming programs. Most importantly, they wanted them to attend school (see Jones 2004). Parents, particularly mothers, began to organize programs for their children inside the schools or outside if necessary. "An example of these early efforts took place in Cuyahoga County, Ohio, in 1933, when five mothers met to express their indignation because their mentally retarded children were excluded from the public schools. From this meeting, the Council for the Retarded was organized. It was successful in establishing a special class to meet the needs of those retarded children who could not adapt to the regular school program" (Segal 1970, 23). Some parents who could not get their children into public schools created their own. Katie Dolan, a mother, describing her educational activism at the time, reported of these schools that mothers "ran them, furnished them, and they found volunteers to teach. I mean these mothers were tough and they got organized" (Schwartzenberg 2004, 14).

Although parent-organized programs gave children some exposure to school, parents realized quickly that systemic changes were needed so that children would be included in public education. Elizabeth Boggs, who was a chemist with a Ph.D. from Cambridge University and the mother of a son with an intellectual disability, became a member of President Kennedy's Panel on Mental Retardation. She explained that parents wanted "something of the same opportunity afforded parents of normal youngsters to received skilled assistance from trained teachers in the rearing of their children," going on to say that "we parents know that we cannot fill this gap alone [because these programs] must be publicly supported in order to

reach all the children who need it" (Jones 2004, 337). Parents began to create what Boggs called "the advance troops of a new consumer movement"
(1994, 47).

By the 1960s, these grassroots parent groups had organized nationally.
For example, the National Association for Retarded Children (NARC, now
known as The Arc), United Cerebral Palsy, and the National Easter Seal
Society all began as parent-initiated childhood disability organizations
(Fleischer and Zames 2000; Pelka 1997). Also during the 1960s, investiga-
tions into state institutions shocked the public with their images of neglect
and abuse. Robert F. Kennedy's critique of conditions of the Rome and
Willowbrook institutions in New York State, Robert Edgerton's description
of conditions in Pacific State Hospital in California, and Burton Blatt and
Fred Kaplan's photographic essay *Christmas in Purgatory*—all contributed to
a growing sense that overcrowded institutions did little but warehouse
people under neglectful and sometimes abusive conditions. NARC and the
Council for Exceptional Children lobbied for rights and services for children
with disabilities, with NARC also developing important ties to the Kennedy
and Johnson administrations (Osgood 2005, 2008). President Kennedy's
creation of the President's Committee on Mental Retardation helped to
refocus public policy regarding people with intellectual disabilities, framing it in terms of individual choice, community-based services, diversity of
differences, equality of opportunities, and humanitarianism (PCMR 1977).

Parents achieved their goals through multiple strategies. One history
of the Arc found that the most effective strategies were personal contact
with public officials, contacts between the associations and public officials, preparation of materials for legislators, letters sent to officials, and
work with civic groups (Segal 1970). On the softer side of advocacy efforts,
mothers in Washington State hosted luncheons for legislators: "'We did it
with love and homemade bread,' said Mrs. Duane (Katie) Dolan, during
the fourth annual Legislator's Luncheon held recently in the Nile temple
at Seattle Center. Katie, publicity chair of the Northwest Center Mothers'
Guild, attributes passage of H.B. 90, mandatory education act for handicapped children, to these luncheons" (Carroll 1971). Parents called their
legislators and invited them personally to these lunches, fed them, and
gave them a ten-minute talk about their goals. They also researched all the
state legislators, finding out who had a family member with a disability or

a family member who had been a teacher or a social worker, and focused particular attention on those representatives (Schwartzenberg 2005).

On the tougher side of advocacy strategies, parents in the 1960s initiated major court challenges to school systems' rejection of their children, using *Brown v. Board of Education* (1954) as a basis for lawsuits questioning the educational exclusion and segregation of their children (Osgood 2005; Scheerenberger 1987). Two key court decisions paved the way for later legislative change. In *Pennsylvania Association for Retarded Children (PARC) v. Commonwealth of Pennsylvania* (1971), "a class action on behalf of all mentally retarded persons, residents of the Commonwealth of Pennsylvania," parents turned to litigation when they were unable to get access to education for their children with intellectual disabilities. In that decision, a federal district court required that all children between the ages of six and twenty-one receive a free public education and stated that "placement in a regular public school class is preferable to placement in a special public school class and placement in a special public school class is preferable to placement in any type of program of education and training." This decision set the precedent for inclusion in public schools and placement of children in the least segregated setting possible.

The next year, in *Mills v. Board of Education of the District of Columbia* (1972), a civil action was brought on behalf of seven African American children of school age who were denied access to education because of disabilities. The decision cites the plaintiff's claim that at the time there were "22,000 retarded, emotionally disturbed, blind, deaf, and speech or learning disabled children, and perhaps as many of 18,000 of these children are not being furnished with programs of specialized education." A District of Columbia Public Schools report for the 1971–1972 school year documented that 12,340 children were not served. In its judgment of this case, the court stated: "The District of Columbia shall provide to each child of school age a free and suitable publicly-supported education regardless of the degree of the child's mental, physical or emotional disability or impairment" and specified detailed parental rights in the placement and service decision-making processes. At the same time parents were using the courts to institute changes, a few states had already started special education systems—Washington (1971), Massachusetts (1972), and Michigan and North Dakota (1973) (Scheerenberger 1987).

Just three years after the Mills decision, in 1975, Congress passed the Education for All Handicapped Act (Public Law 94–142). Described as "the disability movement's equivalent of *Brown v. Board of Education*," the EHA mandated a free, appropriate, integrated public education for all children in the United States, regardless of disability (Shapiro 1994, 166). Parents succeeded in gaining the right for their children to attend public schools, plus procedural rights for parents to participate in the decision-making processes used to determine their children's eligibility and services. This first wave of the disability rights movement created educational opportunities for children and youths with disabilities, then and now. As a result of parental activism, children and youths with disabilities in the United States are now entitled to a public education in the least restrictive environment.

The Independent Living Movement: Disability Discrimination

Adults with physical and sensory disabilities also began to organize before World War II, with the first home office of the National Association of the Deaf in 1880, the Disabled Veterans of America and the National Mental Health Association in 1920, the League of the Physically Handicapped in 1935, and the National Federation of the Blind in 1940 (Young 1997). However, it was not until the 1960s that the independent living movement began, through the activism of young adults with physical (mobility-related) disabilities.

At its inception, the independent living movement was influenced by two social phenomena: post–World War II polio epidemics and the civil rights movement.[3] The first known polio epidemic in the United States occurred in 1894, with major epidemics in 1916 and the worst in 1952 (CDC 2009). These epidemics resulted in a critical mass of young people who had contracted polio and survived. Anne Finger explains the mixed messages that she and other children with polio received at the time: "We shared a common experience of having been told that hard work would enable us to return to the world of the 'normal.' We had heard over and over again about one of us having been president. We were raised in the belief that we could do anything we set our minds to. Great things were expected of us. We then found our way blocked by a myriad of legal obstacles" (Finger 2006, 261). Many of the young leaders of the independent living movement had polio as children, including Judy Heumann, who went on to serve as assistant secretary of education under President Bill Clinton.

In college, students with physical disabilities were inspired by the civil rights movement (and later by the women's and antiwar movements) to push for equal access to educational and employment opportunities. In 1962, four students at the University of Illinois at Champaign-Urbana left a facility to live closer to campus in an accessible home and began to advocate for greater accessibility on campus (Young 1997). A few years later, Ed Roberts, one of the founders of the independent living movement, entered the University of California at Berkeley; by 1967, twelve students with physical disabilities attended college there. These students, who called themselves the Rolling Quads, worked to frame disability issues in terms of independence, and in 1970 were able to obtain a grant from the federal government for a Physically Disabled Students' Program that helped students develop skills to live independently and attend college (NCD 2000; Silver and Wilson 2007). The students who organized this program then took their approach out into the broader community, starting the first Center for Independent Living (CIL) in Berkeley in 1972 (Silver and Wilson 2007). Roberts became the director of the CIL in 1974, then left in 1975 to direct the California Department of Rehabilitation. Ironically, this was the same agency that had determined him to be "unemployable" and therefore ineligible for tuition assistance while he attended the University of California at Berkeley (ibid.).

The independent living movement spurred a new way of thinking about disability. The traditional medical model viewed disability as an individual problem, to be prevented whenever possible and minimized through medical treatment and rehabilitation when it did occur. The independent living movement redefined disability using a social model that saw disability as a societal problem, caused by social practices such as discrimination, segregation, and architectural barriers. From this perspective, people with disabilities were a minority group and civil rights were an important public solution to the social and political barriers they faced.[4] The solutions were to be determined by people with disabilities themselves—they would have consumer control (CIL 1982), giving rise to the slogan, "Nothing about us without us" (Charlton 1998).

Civil rights for people with disabilities were made part of federal policy through Section 504 of the Rehabilitation Act of 1973 (Public Law

93–112). After vetoing it twice, President Richard Nixon signed the act into law on September 26. Section 504, which addressed discrimination against people with disabilities, stated: "No otherwise qualified individual with a disability in the United States, as defined in section 705(20) of this title, shall, solely by reason of her or his disability, be excluded from the participation in, be denied the benefits of, or be subjected to discrimination under any program or activity receiving Federal financial assistance or under any program or activity conducted by any Executive agency or by the United States Postal Service." As others have noted, Section 504 was slipped into the legislation with very little attention or visibility and with no involvement by disability activists (Scotch 1984). Young congressional staffers who were interested in reform and civil rights developed the language, borrowing from the Civil Rights Act of 1964 (Scotch 1984; Shapiro 1994; Switzer 2003; Young 1997).

In his book on Section 504, Richard Scotch describes how "staff members were concerned that, when disabled individuals completed their training in the [vocational rehabilitation] system and were ready to enter the workplace, many employers appeared reluctant to hire them. Staff members felt that the final goal of the VR program, getting disabled people into the mainstream of society, was being blocked by negative attitudes and discrimination on the part of employers and others" (1984, 51). Getting the act passed was only the first of two difficult hurdles. For Section 504 to take effect, the federal government had to issue regulations. These were a long time coming. First there was confusion about which federal agency should have responsibility for the regulations, and then there was reluctance to put them into place, in part due to the estimated cost of compliance (Shapiro 1994). It was not until April 30, 1977, that the U.S. Department of Health, Education, and Welfare (HEW) issued final regulations and the law took effect.

At the same time the regulations were getting bogged down in bureaucracy, adults with physical disabilities were beginning to organize across disabilities, much as parents had in the 1960s. In 1974, Fred Fay, Eunice Fiorito, Judy Heumann, Dianne Latin, Roger Peterson, Al Pimentel, Fred Schreiber, and other activists created the American Coalition of Citizens with Disabilities (ACCD), which began meeting in 1975 (Scotch 1984; Young 1997). Frank Bowe, the first executive director of ACCD, mobilized activists in support of Section 504, bringing a wide range of people with disabilities together for the first time, including "traditional" groups, such as the deaf, and "new" groups, such as paraplegics (Berkowitz 1987).

Early in April 1977, demonstrators protested at the home of the director of HEW and at the national and eight regional HEW offices. The sit-ins got considerable media attention, especially as they dragged on. On the West Coast, Ed Roberts, then the director of the California Department of Rehabilitation, visited the San Francisco sit-in to cheer on the demonstrators, which included Judy Heumann, who protested at the regional HEW office in San Francisco for twenty-five days. An amazing variety of organizations aided the protesters: the Black Panthers delivered Easter dinner, priests celebrated Easter Mass, a rabbi led a Passover Seder, and the Butterfly Brigade (an anti–gay violence group) got walkie-talkies to the protesters (Shapiro 1994). Hundreds of protesters participated in these efforts, galvanizing an adult disability movement.

When HEW finally issued Section 504 regulations in direct response to the movement's pressure, Ed Roberts gave a victory speech in which he described the strength of the movement and the barriers still faced:

> We have begun to ensure a future for ourselves, and a future for the millions of young people with disabilities, who I think will find a new world as they begin to grow up. Who may not have to suffer the kinds of discrimination that we have suffered in our own lives. But that if they do suffer it, they'll be strong and they'll fight back. And that's the greatest example, that we, who are considered the weakest, the most helpless people in our society, are the strongest, and will not tolerate segregation, will not tolerate a society which sees us as less than whole people. But that we will together, with our friends, will reshape the image that this society has of us. (Roberts 1977)

Section 504 strengthened the foundation of civil rights for people with disabilities, building upon the Education for All Handicapped Children Act, which gave children the right to a public education. For example, Section 504 has been used by parents in special education litigation to address discriminatory practices (Martin, Martin, and Terman 1996). This second wave of the disability movement helped create a foundation of civil rights for all people with disabilities. Its scope was restricted, however, to organizations that received federal funds. This left many people with disabilities unprotected from discrimination in the private sector—a gap that would be remedied by the Americans with Disabilities Act more than a decade later.

The Third Wave: Coalitions and Collaboration

In the 1980s, coalitions of disability organizations began to collaborate with disability professionals to advocate for additional changes in disability policy. This collaboration proved fruitful in 1986 during the reauthorization of the Education for All Handicapped Act (EHA), which was renamed later the Individuals with Disabilities Education Act (IDEA). The IDEA changed much of the language in the EHA. Most notably, the word "handicapped" was removed and changed to "disability." Substantively, the IDEA also added a new program, Early Intervention, which provides services to children under the age of three who are diagnosed with or are at risk for having developmental disabilities. Children with disabilities can now receive services meant to maximize their abilities from birth all the way through high school. This potent collaboration of parents and professionals in the disability field worked well, demonstrating the effectiveness of combining parents' voices (telling stories about their children) with professionals' voices (telling what the field of child development thought was best for children).

The Americans with Disabilities Act (ADA) followed several years later, in 1990. It took two years, however, for the ADA to make it through Congress. Two congressmen with personal experiences with disability introduced the bill in 1988: Senator Lowell Weicker, whose son had Down syndrome, and Representative Tony Coelho, who had epilepsy. According to Senator Weicker's statements reported in the *Congressional Record*, he envisioned that the ADA would "establish a broad-scoped prohibition of discrimination and . . . describe specific methods by which such discrimination is to be eliminated" (*Cong. Rec.* 1998, S5107, S5109–110). Built upon what the National Council on Disability calls "twin pillars," the Civil Rights Act of 1964 and the Rehabilitation Act of 1973, the ADA prohibited discrimination against people with disabilities in employment, public services, and public accommodation (Young 1997).

Representative Coelho described the disability movement at that time as a "hidden army" who understood disability because of their own experiences or those of a family member (Shapiro 1994, 117). There were many members of that "hidden army" within Congress: Representative Steny Hoyer's wife had epilepsy; Senator Edward Kennedy's son lost a leg to cancer and his sister had an intellectual disability, Senator Robert Dole had a paralyzed arm due to a war injury, and Senator Orrin Hatch's brother-in-law had polio. President George H. W. Bush was also a member—one son had a learning disability, another son used an ostomy bag due to a colon operation, and an uncle experienced paralysis after contracting polio.

Disability activists collaborated at an unparalleled level. People with disabilities nationwide were encouraged to write "discrimination diaries" documenting their experiences (Mayerson 1993, 21). A total of 180 national organizations sponsored the bill and many participated in the congressional hearings. Witnesses representing organizations such as the Easter Seal Society of Connecticut, American Disabled for Accessible Public Transit (ADAPT, a civil disobedience protest organization that works to improve transportation accessibility), the Disability Rights Education and Defense Fund, the World Institute on Disability (represented by Judy Heumann), the Connecticut Developmental Disabilities Office, the Portland Coalition for the Psychiatrically Labeled, and the Indiana Department of Veterans' Affairs spoke at hearings before the House and Senate as the ADA was shaped and debated. Justin Dart, said to be the "father of the ADA" and "the ADA man" (Fay and Pelka 2003; Fleischer and Zames 2000, 88), described the coalition of advocates behind the ADA, "a ragtag hodgepodge of advocates with disabilities, families, and service providers, who had never completely agreed on anything before, joined together with a few farsighted members of the older civil rights movement, business, the Congress, and the Administration to defeat the richest, most powerful lobbies in the nation."[5] This "hodgepodge" of advocates had its work cut out, as lobbyists for businesses such as construction companies, theatres, and restaurants testified against the ADA, but they succeeded in part due to their united front. The multiple strands of the disability movement—parents of individuals with disabilities, adults with disabilities, and professionals who worked in the disability field—all came together effectively around the ADA.

Although there have been significant challenges to the law's implementation, passage of the ADA is a major achievement of the disability
movement as a whole.[6] At the time, Senator Dole stated: "I have supported
the ADA because I believe it is a just and fair bill, which will bring equality
to the lives of all Americans with disabilities. Our message to America is
that inequality and prejudice will no longer be tolerated. Our message to
people with disabilities is that your time has come" (Young 1997).

The Rules Have Changed

The rules have changed profoundly. Looking back at the past few decades,
it is impressive how much disability activists have achieved. Youths with
disabilities in the United States who are coming of age right now are
the first to grow up under these new rules, which emphasize community-
based education, employment opportunities, and reduced discrimination.
Opportunities have increased and some youths with disabilities transition
to adulthood very successfully in terms of attaining traditional markers
of adulthood, such as completing their education and getting jobs.

3

Participation and Voice

In response to concerns about transition outcomes among youths with disabilities, Congress in 2004 added new requirements to the Individual Education Program (IEP) process through the Individuals with Disabilities Education Act (IDEA). This was an attempt to focus high school special education services on building skills and capabilities that would serve young people once they left school and entered adulthood, rather than simply addressing their educational needs within the high school context. These new requirements mandate that the IEP include "appropriate measurable postsecondary goals" and the "transition services . . . needed to assist the child in reaching those goals."

Congress also made another small addition to the IDEA with transition in mind: it specifically legislated that youths should be able to participate in developing their IEPs, once the focus shifted to transition planning. IDEA regulations now require that "the LEA [Local Education Authority] must invite a child with a disability to attend the child's IEP Team meeting if a purpose of the meeting will be the consideration of the postsecondary goals for the child and the transition services needed to assist the child in reaching those goals" (34 CFR 300.321[b]; 20 U.S.C. 1414[d][1][B]). Massachusetts law takes these federal regulations further: "Students must be invited to all educational meetings and allowed to participate actively when transition planning is discussed."[1]

This idea that youths should have a role in creating their transition plan in high school is brand new. Although small print about IEP meetings

did say previously that the IEP team could also include, "whenever appropriate, the child with a disability," this language did not give youths a concrete right to participate (20 U.S.C. 1414[d][1][B]–[d][1][D]). Instead, it gave
school district staff and parents tremendous discretion in deciding
whether or not to include students in the meetings during which decisions
are made about their educational programs. The adults got to decide if
students' attendance was "appropriate" and if students should be invited
to attend. Today, that discretion ends once transition planning begins—
students must be invited to their IEP meetings at that point.

Congress first gave parents the right to participate in IEP meetings in
special education legislation in 1974. Annual IEP meetings were seen as
joint planning conferences "as the mechanism by which an 'appropriate
education' in the 'least restrictive environment' could be achieved" (Engel
1993, 799). Parents were given a seat at the table where their children's
services for the coming year would be determined. Congress made them a
part of the IEP team, whether schools liked it or not. The IEPs that came out
of these meetings were thus contracts of sorts, which both sides signed to
indicate their agreement regarding what the school would provide to the
student in the following year. If parents did not agree to the plan, they
could refuse to sign it and initiate a mediation and appeals process.

Let's consider the social context into which youths enter if they attend
their IEP transition meetings. Picture a table at which four to twelve adults
are sitting. Youths and parents we interviewed that mothers were always
at the IEP meetings, and about half the time fathers were present too. The
mothers were usually the main family representative, and fathers played a
range of roles, from quiet moral support for mothers to "bad cop" in negotiations. A few parents also brought advocates to the meetings, typically
when they were dissatisfied with the school's approach to addressing their
children's disabilities. In purely physical terms, advocates also helped off-
set the imbalance in numbers, as school staff typically outnumbered parents at the table, sometimes by a wide margin. The school side included
at least one special education administrator, who had the authority to
negotiate with parents and sign off on the IEP, and at least one of the student's teachers. Depending on the level of services being provided to the
student, it also included multiple professionals who worked with the student, such as teachers; speech and language, occupational, and physical

therapists; school nurses; school psychologists; and aides. In rare cases, there could be as many as eight to ten school staff present.

IEP meetings could be uneventful if the parents and school were on the same page. Then they resembled a parent-teacher conference, with the adults discussing the progress the student had made and any needs that still had to be addressed. But meetings could be quite tense if the school contested the student's disability or if there were differences of opinion between parents and staff about the student's needs or the appropriate services to address those needs. Youths who participated in their IEP meetings when they reached transition age therefore stepped into a complex social setting.

Youth Participation

What does it mean for a student to "participate actively" in these meetings, as Massachusetts law provides? Neither IDEA nor Massachusetts special education legislation specifies the content of a youth's participation, leaving tremendous room for interpretation. In fact, youths, like fathers, played a wide range of roles, based on the individuals in my study. Some did not attend their meetings for a variety of reasons, while others attended and played more or less active roles. Youth participation is conceptualized here on a spectrum, in terms of attendance and voice. Attendance is fairly simple—did youths attend their IEP meetings or not? If youths were not present, they were not participating. Voice is more complicated, as youths entered into the discussions to varying extents, adding different kinds of input.

Nonparticipants

I describe the just over one-quarter of young people who did not attend their IEP meetings as nonparticipants. All but three nonparticipants had intellectual disabilities, and about half had multiple disabilities—either intellectual plus physical disabilities or intellectual disabilities in combination with autism. In instances in which youths had intellectual disabilities, parents typically handled all the negotiations during the IEP meetings on behalf of their children, acting as their proxies. Janet, who had two daughters with autism, explained why she had not brought her daughter

Cali to her IEP meetings the year before, when transition planning began: "Cali will attend her first IEP the upcoming year. And the only reason for that, as well, I feel that . . . my girls, they grew up, they know, you know, there's some difference, but they didn't grow up under an umbrella like, 'Oh, I'm autistic.' They didn't grow up with a rubber stamp like, 'Oh, this is . . . ' So for them, you know, it's just like when you talk to kids at certain stages about certain things. You know what I mean?" Janet worried that the autism label could eclipse Cali's perception of her own abilities because of how she heard school staff discussing her condition: "You know, if you hear that you're on the autism spectrum, then it's like you figure, well okay, they have this disability and that disability and that without looking at who it is and what they have." Cali's sister Alex also had autism, but Janet had felt Alex was ready to participate in her IEP meetings at a younger age than Cali, and had held off until she judged Cali mature enough to attend.

None of the nonparticipant youths with intellectual disabilities voiced any concerns about not attending their IEP meetings. They were aware that their parents attended on their behalf and seemed satisfied with that arrangement. Sean said that his parents did go to meetings about transition planning, but that "actually they didn't [me] tell much" about what happened. He knew that his IEP said that his school would prepare him for work after high school—his personal post–high school goal was employment, so he felt that there was little to be concerned about given that his parents and teachers were helping him move toward that goal.

Several youths with learning disabilities were invited to attend their transition planning meetings but declined. They also were satisfied with having their parents advocate on their behalf. Carl had actively resisted participating in his annual IEP meetings because they were held at the public high school where he had experienced severe bullying and resulting anxiety and the school staff refused to hold the meeting at an off-campus location. His local school district had placed him at a private school, in part due to his learning disability but also because of the bullying. His nonparticipation in the meetings was not an important issue for Carl—all that mattered to him was that he didn't have to go to his local high school any longer and that the school district kept sending him to his private school. He was completely happy having his mother speak for him because she had advocated for him successfully. Grace's situation was similar; she was attending a private school for students with learning disabilities and was happy with her school. Although Grace did have an IEP, her mother said that "we never look at it. I mean, it doesn't mean anything." What mattered to Grace and her parents was that the private school was fulfilling Grace's needs and all their expectations, so there was no reason for Grace to participate in the IEP meetings.

Most youths did attend their IEP meetings, though, once transition planning began. If we take attendance at the meetings as the minimum necessary criterion for participation under IDEA, the majority of youths in fact did participate. Almost half of all youths also spoke in some capacity during the meetings, allowing us to add voice to our concept of participation.

Technical Participants

I call the youths who attended IEP meetings but never spoke technical participants. Their bodies were in the room for at least part of the meeting, but they either only listened or sometimes did not even follow the discussion. This group included ten youths, just over one-fifth of all youths with IEPs. In three instances, school staff shaped youths' participation, maximizing it in one case, minimizing it in two others.

Ricardo, who had intellectual and physical disabilities and attended a separate school for students with disabilities in an urban school district, did attend his IEP meetings. He was unable to speak at all and used a word board to make basic requests, but the school staff and his mother felt that it was important for him to be present because he had a legal right to attend. His mother, Maria, explained: "Yes, he was [at the meeting]. I know his right. They bring him and he was a member. The teacher bring him and he was sitting in the wheelchair and the teacher put something like a little kinds of cookie and he was calm and focused and focused on the meeting. . . . He's part of the whole thing, I guess." Ricardo's physical presence in the room was the maximum form of participation feasible for him, and Maria was pleased that his right to attend was honored.

Darren wanted to participate and was prevented from doing so by the adults in the room. He was hard of hearing and wanted to hear and say more during the meetings but could not because he could not hear everyone and the team members did not address him specifically. They spoke to one another, preventing him from being able to follow the discussion. Instead, he "mostly sat and listened," feeling excluded from the conversation about him.

Katherine, who had a physical disability, was excluded more pointedly during her IEP meetings. At home, she used a communication method called "facilitated communication" to speak, in which an assistant helped hold her arm and spell out words on a letter board (a board on which the alphabet is displayed). Use of facilitated communication is very controversial—some say that it enables people with physical disabilities and autism to communicate, while others say that it is the assistant who is really doing the communicating. The school district forbade Katherine to use this technique at school, a ban that extended to the IEP meetings. When the school staff directed questions to Katherine during the meetings, she attempted to answer using facilitated communication but the staff refused to listen to her responses. Katherine said: "I talk, but nobody pays attention. It's not nice to ask someone a question and not listen to their answer." Katherine's mother described Katherine's participation at IEP meetings: "You're going into the shark cage, you're like—she's surrounded." The meetings were very contentious as a result, and during the last IEP meeting the school staff left the room when Katherine and her mother insisted that she be allowed to use facilitated communication to voice her opinions.

Some young people chose to constrain their own participation at times. Four attended the meetings but deliberately chose not to speak for themselves, relying on their parents to advocate for them. Two of them did so because they felt their parents were doing a fine job on their behalf. The first, Anna, a nineteen-year-old with a learning disability, attended part of each of her IEP meetings. Asked if she participated in developing her transition plan, she said: "Well, no. But my parents asked me questions like do I think any large print, or do I think this is helping or something. . . . Because I had a hard time talking to the school about what I needed because I didn't really know unless my parents helped me figure it out." Anna provided input to her parents but then allowed them to take charge in negotiations about services with the school. She was not present for the decision-making part of the meetings, explaining that in the last meeting, "I went to half of it so I could get a sense of what it was about, but then it was so boring that my parents told me not to go to the meeting." The second student who relied on his parents was Craig, who had an intellectual disability. He said that they took care of everything in the meeting. He listened but was not able to remember the specific details that were discussed.

The other two youths chose not to speak in IEP meetings because their parents and the school staff required them to attend but they did not want to be there. Audrey, a seventeen-year-old with a learning disability who had also been labeled with oppositional conduct disorder, attended her IEP meetings in body alone. When asked if she participated in creating her transition plan, she said: "No. I was tired that day. I just sat there . . . my support teachers made the plan." Audrey did not want to acknowledge that she had a disability and did not want to participate in special education. She expressed this in part by refusing to participate more actively in the meetings in which her services were determined. If she had to have services, then it was up to her parents to advocate for them. Damien, who had also been labeled as having behavioral issues, likewise resented having to attend the meetings. He said that the adults talked at, not with, him: "I think everyone has something to contribute to me, like they speak to me at those meetings." His response was to tune out. "I remember one meeting I went to a while ago, I was sitting there and I was really tired, and I just fell asleep like this on the back of this chair. It gets that horrible, I just can't stay awake." For both Audrey and Damien, participation was thrust upon them. They both complied in physical terms, by being in the room during their IEP meetings, but resisted any further involvement.

Vocal Participants

Youths who attended their meetings and spoke at them are labeled vocal participants here, acknowledging that they spoke in some capacity. Most who attended their meetings did speak during them—what varied was the type and length of verbal contributions they made. Most responded to questions posed by the adults in the room as the adults attempted to get their input into the plans being made for them. Some youths prepared vision statements about their futures in advance of the meeting and then shared those visions with the adults present.

The youths' disabilities in part shaped the nature of their vocal participation in the meetings. Most with intellectual disabilities who were vocal participants spoke only when adults posed questions to them. When Lexie, my research assistant, asked Jessica about her IEP transition meeting, Jessica said that her teachers and parents asked her a lot of questions during the meeting, checking in to get her opinion about the decisions being made.

JESSICA: We talked about it in the meeting, about if the IEP was good for me or not. [My teacher] asked me some questions.

LEXIE: Can you tell me a little bit more about that?

JESSICA: Like he asked me some questions about my behavior and stuff, and then like told me about how I need speech, which is how I need to, like, like, about speech which is where they talk to you about thinking, thinking slower, then speaking faster. Sometimes I have trouble speaking faster than I think. I think faster than I speak. So that's where I have trouble.

Jessica had felt included in the meeting and liked the plan developed for her because it focused on her goal of pursuing a career in culinary arts.

Mary, who was twenty years old and had an intellectual disability, described her meetings as fairly informal: "My mom comes to school to meet my teacher. My mom comes in and they do my IEP meeting with my school, we have a little chat, visit my teacher." When asked about her transition plan, she said that she didn't remember what was in it: "My teacher knows all that." Mary's mother, Melinda, explained that they had to facilitate Mary's participation: "We'll ask her questions, 'You want to do this or that?' She doesn't have a lot of role. It's very hard for her to make a connection between that kind of meeting and what she does all day long. We can ask, 'Do you want to take this course or that course?' She'll respond to that. . . . If we said, okay, do you want to do math, she'd say, 'No.' [*Laughs.*] Sometimes you just don't ask." William's parents and teachers also facilitated his participation as much as possible. His mother explained: "He's been there. And when he is there, the conversation is much slower. So he has played a role. He has said, I like music, I like to cook, I like this. But beyond that, we have to do a lot of kind of scaffolding to help in choices." William did report playing a role in the meetings and answering questions, but from his perspective, much of the conversation consisted of the adults in the room urging him to become more involved in the process of planning his future. This urging was echoed in William's description of the meetings and his transition plan.

WILLIAM: They say I should take some responsibility.

LEXIE: Did they talk about responsibility?

WILLIAM: Yes.

LEXIE: Did they say responsibility with what?

WILLIAM: With disabilities.

LEXIE: Were they talking about when you go to live somewhere after high school? Were they talking about that kind of responsibility?

WILLIAM: Yes.

LEXIE: Do you remember what they said about living?

WILLIAM: Yeah.

LEXIE: What did they say about that?

WILLIAM: They say that I should go about my business.

LEXIE: . . . Did they talk about it after high school?

WILLIAM: Yes.

LEXIE: What did they say about that?

WILLIAM: They say that I should be more flexible.

LEXIE: Be more flexible?

WILLIAM: Yeah.

LEXIE: Be more flexible with what?

WILLIAM: With playing music and things.

When pressed about the specific content of his transition plan:

WILLIAM: They want me to be excited.

LEXIE: They want you to be excited?

WILLIAM: Yes.

LEXIE: About finishing high school?

WILLIAM: Yes.

LEXIE: Are you excited?

WILLIAM: Yeah.

The kind of scaffolding that William's mother described as necessary during the meeting was mirrored in the interview. William had definite opinions about what he did and did not want to do—he wanted to continue playing music and liked cleaning kitchens as a job. But he voiced his opinions only when prompted to do so, and then in fairly narrow terms. (The other parts of William's interview were much more conversational, especially about his plans to live with roommates after finishing school. It was questions about his IEP transition plan at school that elicited this limited back and forth.)

The transition meeting provided an opportunity for school staff and parents to check in with youths about their future plans in a more formal way. According to the young people, most of the questions that adults posed during the meeting were about what they wanted to do after high school. Essentially, adults asked youths the perennial question that plagues young people from preschool age through college (and sometimes beyond): "What do you want to be when you grow up?" Youths with all types of disabilities reported being asked during their IEP meetings about their vision of the future and their specific goals—there were no differences by type of disability. In Massachusetts, schools are supposed to complete a formal, written transition plan, which is seen as part of the IEP. The youths' postsecondary goals are spelled out at the beginning of the transition plan and described as their "vision." The needs and services specified in the latter parts of the transition plan are supposed to be based upon this vision of where youths want to go after high school.

Frederick, who had Asperger syndrome, participated in his transition IEP meetings on a limited basis. At the end of one meeting, he was asked about his vision of the future and made a statement about himself and his goals. His mother Patti was thrilled, describing it as "a speech like a rabbi—everybody cried." When Lexie asked Frederick about whether he participated in creating his IEP, he said that he did not and explained that "they don't need me for until the last couple of minutes when they've come up with the nitty-gritty." His role was to provide the vision. His mother and the school staff negotiated the details about how the school would support this vision. Frederick was happy with his transition plan (which specified that he was college bound), with his high school, and with the level of input he had into the process of creating his plan.

Laura, who had an intellectual disability, described how the adults in the meeting asked her about what she wanted to do with the rest of her life:

LAURA: They all like to talk to me about what do you want to do when you grow up and all that kind of stuff at the meetings. . . . What do you want to do when you grow up, and what do you want to do outside of [school]. That's what they talk about. . . .

LEXIE: So have you told them what you want to do?

LAURA: I told—yeah, I keep on telling them what I want to do when I get out of [high school]. I've been telling them that I want to be a day-care person, and I want to help little kids that have special needs. You know, not kids in wheelchairs and that kind of stuff, because I really don't want to get run over with wheelchairs. I just want to work with little kids who have special needs and maybe help them with stuff. So it's really kind of cool to do that. So I really want to do that. So it'd be kind of cool.

William, Frederick, and Laura all had fairly specific visions of what they would like their lives to be like after leaving high school.

Youth who were less certain of the pathways they wanted to take into adulthood reported being cajoled into thinking more seriously about their plans for the future during their IEP transition meetings. Ophelia, who had Asperger syndrome, also said that the adults in her meeting asked her about what she wanted to do after high school. "I said that I'd like something with animals or writing or something. I don't exactly remember what I said then, because I know my opinions have changed since then. But I still want to do stuff with writing and animals." Kaiser, who also had Asperger syndrome, was asked if he'd spoken at his IEP meetings:

KAISER: Sort of, yeah. A bit. Not a whole lot, but, yeah, I have.

LEXIE: Have they asked you at all what you'd like to do after you finish high school?

KAISER: Yes.

LEXIE: And can I ask what you told them, if you don't mind?

KAISER: Same thing that I told you, pretty much.

LEXIE: So the photography and the dog training?

KAISER: Yeah.

Kaiser's vision of his future at this point extended just to the type of work that he might enjoy doing. He admitted he wasn't entirely sure about what he would do after high school, so being asked about it during his transition meeting prompted him to think more seriously about his future and the kind of job he wanted.

Being asked about their visions of the future spurred some youths to participate more actively in the entire discussion about their futures, resulting in occasional sparks of independence and rebellion. When Chico, a youth with an intellectual disability, was asked if he talked during his IEP meetings, he explained that he talked about the jobs he was interested in doing after high school.

CHICO: The adults really talked more, really. I just said, like, a few things, but that's about it.

LEXIE: Okay. So when you talked about jobs, what kind of jobs did you talk about?

CHICO: She, my teacher, did say that she does know I like cooking, but she wanted me to say, to say it. And you know what I did besides that, so I said why not, like—Oh yeah, she also said, like—She also knew I like drawing, drawing cartoons. . . . I said maybe, like, I can work at a mall, maybe working at a—maybe being a cashier or whatnot at the mall. I gave her some cool store, Hot Topic [a store selling youth clothing, including jeans, gothic and grunge wear, lingerie, and music t-shirts].

LEXIE: Oh.

CHICO: She says, "Why do you want to go there?" I said, "I like—I like the clothes there, and the people there scared my mom."

Missy, who also had an intellectual disability, was asked at her transition meeting about her vision of the future. She began to describe what she wanted her life to be like after high school and played an increasingly active role in the subsequent conversation.

MISSY: We talked about how I want to go college . . . and how I want to live with my family, and all that. And how I do all that stuff before I leave [high school], and stuff.

LEXIE: Did your mom talk at the meeting at all, or your dad?

MISSY: My mom did. I don't know if my dad did. I don't think—he tries to, but I don't know if he got anything in, because my mom usually does all of the talking and he doesn't really get anything in.

LEXIE: [*Laughs.*] What did your mom talk about, if you remember?

MISSY: About the summer. . . . But my mom came—I mean, my mom made up her own vision, and I made up my own vision.

LEXIE: What did your vision say?

MISSY: My vision said [working], living with my family. Living with my family. Living, maybe having an apartment with my best friends and taking the dog—having the dog live with me. My mom didn't like that idea. She was at the meeting. She heard that. She's like, "No, I'm taking her." I was like, "We'll see about that," because we wanted to take her. And she didn't like that idea that I wrote that. I was like, "Well, it's what I wrote."

LEXIE: So what did your mom's vision say?

MISSY: Just stuff that she wants me to work on and stuff like that.

LEXIE: Can you remember certain things that she wanted you to work on?

MISSY: Like reading and [occupational therapy] and [communication therapy], they're most important things she wanted me to work on.

Once Missy was asked for her opinions, she continued to share them during the meeting, even when she knew that they conflicted with her mother's views. Missy's mother, Cassandra, had been a very strong and vocal advocate for Missy for many years. She described herself as a hard-nosed advocate for her daughter. She said that her husband was there for her: "He supports me and comes to the IEPs. But I'm the one that does it, you know what I mean?" Cassandra wanted Missy to be involved in the meetings but was concerned that all the adult attention distracted Missy to some extent from what needed to happen in the meeting. Unlike most youths, who cringed under the adult attention, Missy was a flower basking in the sun during her meetings. Cassandra explained: "So Missy's just like, 'Oh, my God, this is heaven! The attention's on me, and I'm in the middle of all the people that care about me.' So she's not focusing in on what's happening in that meeting, you know what I mean?" Cassandra felt as though the responsibility for negotiating was placed firmly on her shoulders.

Missy's enjoyment of her IEP meetings was very unusual. Most youths preferred not to be in the spotlight. They viewed it more as a hot seat, an interrogation of sorts. Joseph, who had a learning disability, had a bad experience in his previous IEP meeting and was justified in disliking them. The school staff had gone after him, criticizing him directly for his lack of academic progress in the previous year. According to Joseph and his mother, the school had not provided him with appropriate services for his learning disability and attempted to shift blame from themselves to Joseph. As a result of the school's inaction, Joseph's family was able to justify getting him moved to another school where his needs were being met. Even though the school staff would be completely different at his next IEP meeting, Joseph still did not want to attend or participate in the discussion: "I'd actually like to say nothing. That would be my goal. [Laughs.] I don't know. I don't think I'm going to try to talk. I'll see what's said, then determine if I need to talk." Joseph would be happier having his mother speak for him, after the upset of last year's meeting.

Rose, who had Asperger syndrome, wasn't comfortable attending her IEP meetings either. When she was asked if she goes to the meetings, she responded:

ROSE: Occasionally, but it always feels awkward.

LEXIE: Why?

ROSE: Well, a bunch of people are talking about me and I know they all expect different things from me and sometimes I feel like they're discussing something I don't want to know, behind my back.

LEXIE: So when you say that everyone expects something different of you, can you elaborate a little more?

ROSE: Like the aide might want me to succeed in education. My parents obviously want me to have good social skills. My social worker might want me to succeed so it looks good when people view his career, that sort of thing.

When Lexie asked her if she helped to create her IEP, Rose said that she had to do mission statements once she got old enough. They involved writing out her goals for that year. Her mother, Nellie, explained:

NELLIE: She knows everyone at the meetings. And she'll talk a little bit and listen. What did she say at last year's—it was kind of odd for her to be there, because she's been there—she started when she was fourteen, fifteen. Yeah, I think fifteen—anyway, a couple of years back. And I remember looking up [and she said], "It's kind of odd to be here." That's how she put it. And it was. I mean, it's very different from seeing your teachers or guidance counselor or whomever—situation—this is people talking about you. And she's talking about her—and for years it would be something I did or Ben and I did, and she wasn't aware of what an IEP was then. I think it was when I had her read her IEP.

VALERIE: Is it helpful, do you think, to have her come and participate?

NELLIE: Not particularly. It's more a matter of would it help her see that people are actually advocating for her. Not so much that she can provide any insight. They ask her, "How are things going for you?" and she'll say, "Fine." I mean, she won't have any background to say more than things are okay or things aren't okay. I mean, what else can a sixteen-year-old kid say except, "I like this class," or "I don't like that class," whatever. It's more, these people are here to advocate for you and to listen to you. So that's not bad.

From Rose's perspective, it felt uncomfortable to be the center of so much attention. Although she did attend the meetings and write her mission statements and answer questions, she didn't feel welcome at the meetings. She felt like an interloper, even though she was the sole and explicit focus of the discussion. Rose's interpretation of her participation was in line with her mother's account: while Rose had the right to voice her opinions, her role was a minor one once the IEP team got down to negotiating the nitty-gritty, and they were in fact talking about her without her.

Even when youths did participate more actively in the meeting, there was no guarantee that they would be happy with the result of their efforts to advocate on their own behalf. Alan, who had an intellectual disability, had participated quite a bit in his last IEP meeting but felt that the adults were not really listening to him. When he was asked if he helped to make his transition plan, he replied:

ALAN: *They* kind of did.

LEXIE: So was it kind of like they asked you if you wanted to do it?

ALAN: Yes. . . . Well, I kind of got mad because, I don't know, I really don't know if this is the job I want. Because the job I really want—I get disgusted, well, not disgusted, but I just wasn't that happy after that IEP meeting. It really took me really hard.

Alan wanted to work with cars, but it wasn't clear if he would be able to get his driver's license. He was also interested in horticulture, but the school had put him into a culinary arts program for the past three years, where he was unhappy. From his perspective, the school was putting him where they

wanted him to be and did not listen to him when he expressed his interests and opinions about his future.

Hannah, who also had an intellectual disability, wanted a greater
voice in her meetings. Although she attended part of them, she wasn't sure
how she and her opinions fit in. When Hannah was asked about her work
goals after high school, she replied: "Well, they didn't talk about that yet.
I want to, but I don't know who I'm going to talk to about that." The IEP
meetings were the place where these questions about the future were
typically addressed, but Hannah was not aware of that. When Hannah's
mother, Jean, was asked if Hannah attended her IEP meetings, she said:
"She does. I mean, it's fine if she comes, but I would just as soon if she's not
there half the time because I like to get down to the, you know, well, she's
really not doing this or she's doing this. You know what I mean? It's difficult to do all this in front of your kids. You know, I just took her to the doctor and said, 'Could you have the doctor call me, because I want to discuss
some things [about sex and birth control] that I really don't want to discuss
in front of her.'" Hannah confirmed that she was not involved much in the
discussion during IEP meetings, saying that "usually, my mom talks."

The exact nature of youths' vocal participation could shift over time as
they attended multiple annual meetings. Isabella, who had an intellectual
disability, started attending her IEP meetings when she was fourteen. Her
mother said that Isabella attended her first IEP meeting because she wanted
to "make sure she was going to be moving up to the high school. She didn't
want to stay in the middle school, so she came in and technically, yeah,
because they have to come. You can invite them at fourteen." At that first
meeting, Isabella attended but didn't talk—her goal was to make sure that
her parents advocated successfully to have her moved up to her local
high school. At her last IEP meeting, Isabella said that she and her mother
attended and that they talked about her going to the local Arc for services,
indicating that she had been part of the discussion. Participation could be a
developmental effort in this and other instances—youths' roles became more
active with increased exposure and experience attending their IEP meetings.

Empowered Participants

Five youths were actively involved in their IEP meetings in terms of both
discussion and decision making. These empowered participants, as I call

them here, did not just make statements about their visions of the future and respond to questions during meetings but participated in drafting material for their transition plans in advance of the meetings, allowing them to take part in developing all aspects of the plan before coming into the more formal IEP meeting setting with the school staff. Empowered participants were involved in the negotiations about the services that they would receive in the coming year, unlike vocal participants. Behind each empowered youth was an adult who deliberately mentored him or her into taking on a self-advocacy role.

Justin, who had a physical disability, had attended his IEP meetings for several years and felt that there was a real difference between his earlier IEP meetings and the ones that now focused on transition issues: "IEP meetings you don't really care about, because they—they ask you, 'Hey, what do you want to do when you grow up?' and you say, 'I want to be this and that,' and that's the end of your input. But the transition meeting's very important. They ask you everything from, 'Okay, do you want to go school?' 'Where do you want to live?' 'How do you want to do this?'" Part of this difference was the transition focus of the meetings. A key part of the shift in Justin's experience was that he gained a mentor who helped him develop his transition plan before the meeting and facilitated his participation during the meeting. He felt very close to his mentor, who was an adult who also had a physical disability and was a professional in the disability field. Justin explained that "she was the person that kept me hanging on." She helped him understand the purpose of the transition plan and think through what he wanted to do after high school and the services that his school should provide to prepare him for that life. Justin explained that she "did a good job of saying, 'Okay, we're going to basically put your life down on paper for the next three years.' She didn't say this in front of them [the rest of the IEP team] because it would offend a bunch of people. When we were alone, she said, 'This is about you, so it's not about what Doctor Jones thinks or your mom thinks. They can have their input, and if you like what they said then you can have that.'"

Justin remained an active participant throughout his IEP transition-planning meeting, along with the adults who were involved in his life and schooling at the time. He explained that "it was a bunch of us," and it was "a team effort." Justin and his mother were there, as were three staff members from his school and his mentor. When I asked what role he played in the meeting, he responded: "I played a big part. If I didn't like what people were saying, I'd say, 'I don't like what it says about my doing this,' and [the school staff member] would be like, 'Okay, let me word it differently.' I'd be like, 'I still don't like it.' [*Laughs.*]" Justin was one of two youths who had his own copy of his IEP and transition plan and offered to show them to us during our discussion. He was proud of them, having played such an active role in producing them.

Kayla was the other youth who had her own copy of her transition plan. She was the only female who was an empowered participant, and the only empowered youth with an intellectual disability. Three of the five had physical disabilities, and the fourth had Asperger syndrome. Kayla was mentored into this active role by her aunt, with whom she lived. Kayla came to live with her aunt and uncle after she was eighteen and they did not seek legal guardianship of her, so under special education law she was an adult and could participate in the meetings and sign her own IEP and transition plan. Her aunt decided not to obtain signing rights for Kayla, and instead mentored Kayla into taking the primary advocacy role herself. Kayla explained that she participated in writing the plan and in negotiations during her IEP meeting:

KAYLA: I got a chance to talk and my aunt helped me with it, that's why it says shared decision making. And that was my aunt and I, so we kind of did that.

LEXIE: So you actually got to help—you know, tell them what you wanted to do and stuff?

KAYLA: Yeah. Those are my—this is—yeah, this one was April twenty-fourth, this was the last year.

Kayla pulled out her copy of the IEP during her interview so that she could show what was in it, including her goals to do culinary work after high school. Kayla's aunt, Kelsey, explained that it did take substantial work to help Kayla prepare for her IEP meetings: "Kayla has to take notes. She has to write down what she wants and then she has to read them. And I actually make her read them. I actually tell her, 'Kayla, read what's on the paper.' Because once she gets there, she becomes intimidated. And so if she reads what's on the paper, even if she just looks at the paper and just reads it, at least they're her words and not just mine. Because they made it very clear that I have no authority. And it's true. I have no authority." Kelsey positioned herself as a mentor, helping Kayla speak for herself. This mentoring extended not just to IEP meetings, but also to preparing for doctor visits. Kelsey was engaged in a kind of scaffolding, not unlike what William's mother described, but she took it a step further by requiring that Kayla do the advocacy work herself during IEP transition meetings, albeit with support.

Kelsey did establish some limits on Kayla's decision-making capacity, however, due to her intellectual disability. She was concerned that school staff might be able to get Kayla to sign papers that were not in her own interest. So although Kayla did sign her IEP for herself, she did so under adult supervision, Kelsey said.

We had it put on the IEP that she is not to sign anything until another nonschool staff person or family member looks at it. And we had it done that way so that [local social service agency], her social worker, somebody else could read through it with her. It didn't have to be me. . . . And it's not just me, so they can't say, well, you're here, will you sign it now. So, it's any staff, anybody can sign it. Anybody can review it. *You* can review it. As long as there was another adult to review it with Kayla. . . . And it's an adult saying, sign this. Kayla has a hard time standing up to certain people, espe-cially women who exude a certain point of authority. You know, if you're really laid back, she has no problem standing [up for herself], but if you're a person who exudes authority. Like the principal tends to wear a power suit, and if the principal handed her a piece of paper and said, "Sign it," she'd sign it. If I said, "Kayla, sign it," she might tend to waver a little bit. So this way we have the safeguard that somebody else has to look at it, somebody who is not a school person.

All the empowered youths had some scaffolding in place. It was that scaffolding which allowed them to play such active roles in developing and negotiating their transition plans. There were two differences in Kayla's case. First, she was legally entitled to sign her IEPs because she was over eighteen years of age, while the other youths' IEPs had to be signed by their parents. Second, her intellectual disability required her aunt to do more scaffolding work than the mentors did for the empowered youths who did not have intellectual disabilities.

The other three empowered youths were boys who were mentored by their mothers and were college bound. When we asked Teddy, who had Asperger syndrome, about who wrote his transition plan, he explained that he, his parents, and staff at his school all contributed to it. Both he and his mother said that they cowrote the vision statement on the plan, which specified that he was preparing for college entry. Teddy explained: "I guess you could say I built it, now they support it, if you want to say that." He felt good about the plan, and said that it fit his goals completely, even spelling out some honors work that he would do in preparation for college.

Frankie, who had a physical disability, described himself as "an active and willing participant in conversations about [transition]. All things pertaining to my well-being." He, his mother, an advocate, and six school staff participated in his IEP meetings. Like Teddy's, Frankie's vision was to attend college. His mother, Celie, reported that Frankie's high school had not been very helpful on transition issues: "They'll be like, 'What's your five-year goal,' or whatever. I mean, they're helping a little bit with getting an evaluation for assistive technology, with that Dragon software. But otherwise, no, they haven't been very helpful." The school had not talked with them about a transition plan, even though Frankie was only two years away from leaving high school. In Celie's opinion: "They just want to cut him loose when he's eighteen and stop paying for him. Yeah, that's their plan, get rid of him as fast as possible. [*Laughs.*]" Celie was getting advice on transition from a friend who was a professional in the disability field who also had a son with a physical disability. She and Frankie were working with their advocate to push the school system to provide services that would support Frankie's goal to attend college. Frankie reported that he and his mother were very close and worked as a team.

Steve, who also had a physical disability, also worked closely with his mother. They had been thinking through the skills he would need to attend college and live more independently. Steve described his last IEP meeting, in which "they kind of just threw their ideas up there, but I kind of just told them what I really wanted to do." Nine people attended the meeting: Steve, both parents, an advocate, and five school staff (his paraprofessional, his physical therapist, the school nurse, the assistant principal, and his math teacher). Steve's mother, Rita, said that she and her husband had worked on a vision of Steve's future, and that Steve had written his own version of the vision statement in advance of the meeting. She said: "So we did do a transition, and it was pretty much like the vision. He attends the team meetings, so it was a vision statement from us, a vision from him. . . . Well, that's his vision, yes, and we've just been supportive of that vision. I think with the transition phase, our big piece is the physical transition. I mean, we know that academically, we're trying to step back with the paraprofessional help in the class, trying to find things that maybe are easier. Like with technology, something he can carry with him. Something maybe even lighter than a laptop that he could carry in a folder."

Steve's parents' vision focused on how the school would help him develop specific skills that would allow him to be more independent in college, such as using a computer for taking notes. Steve understood that he needed more independent skills and wanted to attend a summer program that worked on them. The school staff had other ideas about how he should spend the summer months, he said.

STEVE: They're trying to get me to stay around here and work with the little kids at the high school, because we have a preschool in our high school. But I kind of wanted to go to the [summer program for youth with disabilities] where I'd have a lot of my friends. I'm not saying I have most of my friends there. I have a lot of friends here, too. But I have lots of my friends that I'd like to see.

LEXIE: So you only see them in the summer.

STEVE: Yeah. And I had to come up with real reasons for me to go there, like beneficial reasons, and I said I'd probably be able to get stronger and become more independent by going there. So I kind of used those reasons why I should go there. But they were trying to get me to stay here and work with little kids. And I had to say it wasn't going to be beneficial enough.

Steve felt that he would gain more independent living skills in the program, which would help him once he went to college. Even in the face of opposition from the school staff, Steve held fast to what he wanted to do and advocated for himself during the service negotiation phase of the transition meeting.

Voice and Power

Youths and parents typically had mixed feelings at best about IEP meetings. Youths' participation in the IEP meetings added yet another layer to an already complex process. This was particularly true when youths were present but did not participate actively. It was not always clear to them why they were there or exactly what was happening, and it was often uncomfortable to be surrounded by adults talking about them.[2] Parents at times felt as though their attention was divided between the advocacy work they needed to do in the meeting, and the additional organizational and emotional work that they needed to do to include their children in the discussion. Kelsey, Kayla's aunt, admitted that it was challenging for her to mentor Kayla into taking such an active role in the transition meetings: "I want what she wants. And she doesn't know what she wants." Kelsey saw her primary role as helping Kayla figure out what she wanted. Ursula, Joseph's mother, said that at Joseph's old school, "they would always say he has to self-advocate. He has to be more independent. I said, 'For God's sake, he doesn't even know what to self-advocate for!' I said, 'I'm just figuring out what he should self-advocate. What do you suggest he self-advocates for? He doesn't know what to ask for.'" Victoria, whose son Trevor had Asperger syndrome, felt similarly: "The last [meeting] was the first one that he was invited to and he just sat there and they're like, 'Do you agree to this, Trevor?' And he's like, 'Yep.' I don't think he has any idea. And you know what? Us as parents really have no idea. I mean—" Her husband Jeffrey cut in: "You can't decipher them. You need information on that too. They don't tell you actually what you can have and what you can't have and try to give the minimal that you can have." Ursula, Victoria, and Jeffrey all found it hard to help their children advocate for themselves when they felt that they themselves were still figuring out how to advocate effectively. This didn't stop them from trying, and learning as a family.

It is true that most youths and young adults do not have the skills to negotiate with adults about their services. Yet adults, both school staff and parents, helped maintain young people's lack of experience when they excluded youths from preparing for their IEP transition meetings and from participating in the decision-making phase of the meetings. Ironically, parents were aware that school staff sometimes made decisions and then presented those decisions to them during the meetings for their approval, without including the parents in the process of producing the decisions. A study in the 1990s of parents' participation in IEP meetings found that "parents themselves feel intimidated and excluded from the decision-making process. They feel that their views carry little weight in comparison to the views of professionals and that their participation is primarily symbolic. . . . Although they are present at the meetings *because* they are laypersons and *because* they are the child's parents, these become the very reasons why, in their view, their participation has little effect on the IEP conference" (Engel 1993, 800–801, emphasis in original). The author noted that parents "sense that 'they' [school staff] are in control and that they do things 'to' rather than 'with' the parents" (802) and that "the basic statutory premise of parental participation has not, from the parents' perspective at least, been realized in practice" (801).

Parents were typically not aware when they helped perpetuate a similar dynamic by restricting their children's participation in much the same ways that school staff sometimes restricted their own participation. This power dynamic of insiders versus outsiders played out in instances when youths felt that their presence and voice were not needed, even though the purpose of the meetings was to discuss and plan their own future. This time it was adults versus youths, rather than school staff versus parents. Rose felt this way—she thought that adults were talking about her behind her back and it made her uncomfortable. Damien felt that the adults were talking at him, not with him, at the meetings. Other youths were allowed to opt out of their meetings, while parents would never have opted out themselves—parents' presence was seen as necessary, while youths' was not. Most youths were content with minimal participation. They typically perceived the meetings to be boring at best and tense and full of conflict at worst, so they weren't pushing for greater participation.

With few exceptions, these parents would be disturbed to think that they had shortchanged their children's development or participation. In fact, if students knew about their right to participate, they learned it from their parents. But parents' primary goal was effective advocacy for their children—if they got what they thought their children needed, that was real success. Parents were largely unaware of the direct power they had over their children's participation. Youths' participation in transition meetings was a secondary goal, if it was a goal at all; it was eclipsed by parents' concern about advocating effectively with the schools on behalf of their children, representing their children's best interests as they perceived them. Parents could facilitate youths' full participation, make room for partial participation, or exclude them altogether. Parents' actions to minimize their children's participation usually were made with the very best of intentions—to avoid their getting bored or being placed in a uncomfortable situation. Yet these actions and intentions reduced their children's participation.

Is youths' participation merely symbolic? From the experiences reported here, the answer is a resounding no. Youths learned from their participation. They drafted vision statements of their future, which encouraged them to think about what they wanted from adult life and how their school might help them achieve those dreams and goals. They talked with their parents about what they needed and voiced their opinions during their IEP meetings. A few youths got practice advocating for themselves directly, taking part in making decisions about their lives rather than leaving it to adults to make decisions on their behalf.

The handful of empowered youths who participated as a team with adults who mentored them were unusual not just because they shared advocacy work in the meetings, but because they understood that the meetings were shaping their future opportunities. What distinguished these youths was not the nature of their disability, but that an adult in their lives deliberately used the meetings as a means of mentoring them into advocating for themselves. These adults understood that their children's participation was not necessarily going to happen quickly or even easily, but they wanted to start the process of teaching these skills before youths left high school, building their development as self-advocates. These adults were typically parents, but other adults could transmit these skills too. Empowered youths' participation in their IEP transition-planning meetings would seem to fulfill the disability rights rallying cry quoted earlier: "Nothing about us without us."

4

Making Their Own Maps

The youths in this study expressed desires about their future destinations, but the routes that they would take to achieve their goals were not always clear to them. Having a dream, a desired destination, was not enough. They needed direction. Few road maps took into account obstacles or complications associated with their disabilities that they might experience. The presence of a disability added another layer of complexity to planning for life after high school, although the thickness of that layer varied considerably depending upon the nature and severity of a youth's disability. Unlike other youths, those with disabilities may also need to learn about their rights under federal disability laws, namely Section 504 of the Rehabilitation Act of 1973 and the Americans with Disabilities Act, and how to use those rights in school and work. For example, youths who wanted to attend college might need to learn about disability services and supports available through their prospective schools. Youths with intellectual disabilities and their families also had to learn new rules—adult service systems are entirely separate from special education, with their own eligibility criteria, funding, and priorities for service delivery. Contemporary youths with disabilities may have higher expectations than did those of previous generations, so successful pathways into adulthood may be largely uncharted. Social capital was the key to getting the direction they needed.[1]

One way of describing social capital is as "a particular kind of resource available to an actor," a social resource that is "productive, making possible the achievement of certain ends, that in its absence would not be possible" (Coleman 1988, S98). For youths with disabilities leaving high school, social capital takes the form of resources gathered through social connections that have the potential to shape youths' life trajectories into adulthood. Young people and their parents produced social capital through their interactions with formal and informal social structures, such as schools, disability organizations, state agencies, and networks of other individuals. Some youths and families were connected with a wide range of individuals and organizations that offered social capital, while others had relatively few social resources. Youths' social connections, both directly and through their parents, shaped their awareness of opportunities available to them.[2]

Friends were important sources of social support for these youths. However, while a majority talked with their friends about the future (68 percent), much of that support was emotional in nature. Friends rarely provided social capital, except among college-bound youths who had friends who were a year or more ahead of them in school. One of Grace's best friends, for example, had started working on college preparation with a guidance counselor at their private school, and the friend was sharing her knowledge with Grace. "I just try to get information from her," Grace said, about SAT preparation and college choices that would provide good supports for her learning disability.

Parents as Central Conduits of Social Capital

Adults, especially parents, were the main conduits of social capital for youths. When asked whom they had talked with about the future over the past year, every one mentioned at least one of their parents. Laura, who had an intellectual disability, felt that her parents "support me in every way." Most youths (80 percent) mentioned both their mother and their father—all but two who lived in intact families said that they talked with both parents. (The other two talked with their mothers only.) Steve said conversations about the future happened regularly with his parents, and informally: "Usually when something pops into my mind, I usually talk to them about it before I forget it. . . . It's not like, 'Oh, on Thursday we're going to have a planned discussion about—' and then they'll sit down with you and you tell them what you want to do with your life." With few exceptions, youths felt that their parents were entirely supportive of whatever they wanted to do with their lives. Frederick explained that his parents "just expect me to have a very strong successful career doing what I love. Of course, that's as cliché as it is, so all I can really do is just make the best of whatever life throws at me." A few exceptions were youths who felt that parents were standing in their way—this occurred in several instances when youths wanted careers that parents felt were unlikely to allow them to be self-supporting, such as wrestling or acting. These parents wanted their children to develop a backup plan in case their dream jobs did not work out.

Such tensions with parents are not unusual for teenagers and young adults, but disability issues could sometimes create additional challenges. Justin, who had a physical disability, explained that being dependent on his parents could be difficult: "We don't want to go to the movie with our parents, just like everyone else, but it's a little harder. Our parents have to be there because we maybe need help or something like that. I did a lot of that, letting the parents know that it's normal to hate you." Kevin also mentioned tension with his mother, saying that although they were very close, "at this time, my mother doesn't want to let me go and I want to go as far as possible and it's difficult to do that when you live under the same roof. So we've both been working on her to stop getting into me and asking me if I did my homework. But I've also had to ask for help and that's sort of hard to do." Disability issues sometimes kept youths somewhat dependent on their parents at a time when their peers without disabilities were becoming more independent.

Mothers and fathers did not always play equal supporting roles. Elaine felt closer to her mother than her father "because my dad and I are so alike that we tend to butt heads." Sandy felt the opposite way: he felt closer to his father because they had more interests in common. He said that he loved his mother, but "lately I've felt somewhat distant toward her, probably because of the whole teenager mentality." Youths who mentioned their mothers but not their fathers (20 percent) were almost all in their mothers' custody as the result of a divorce. Carl's parents were divorced, and he explained that while he was very close to his mother, "I don't talk to my dad much." Mona, who did not see much of her father because he lived in another state, described her mother as "my best friend and I love her more than anything in the world." A handful of youths with divorced parents were living with stepfathers, but none mentioned their stepfathers when asked whom they talked with about the future.

Parents were not only an important source of emotional support but also the main source of social capital for youths as they planned their entry into adulthood. Families are key social contexts for any youths, particularly during the transition to adulthood, and can have important effects on their children's development.[3] In this instance, parents produced social capital through their relations within formal and informal social structures, such as schools, disability organizations, state agencies, and networks of other individuals. Parents provided the foundation for youths' planning efforts, particularly when they reached out to other parents of youths with disabilities and to community-based organizations where resources existed. Parents built rich resource networks that provided information about college, employment, and independent living arrangements.

Youths did not typically do this investigative work themselves and gave parents credit when they were aware that they were doing it for them, such as when their parents helped them seek employment. For example, five youths mentioned specifically that their mothers had helped find jobs for them. Craig's mother found him a cashier job at Stop 'n' Shop on Saturdays. He said: "I wanted to work, so my mom got me that job." Sergeant's mother got him a janitorial job at their synagogue. Jessica got some cleaning jobs for local families, and Audrey had gotten a job taking photographs with Santa Claus at a local mall the previous Christmas. When asked how she got the job, Audrey replied: "Actually, my mom found out about it and asked me if it was something I'd be interested in and I said yes." Donnie's mother got him a stocking job at Marshalls, which he enjoyed. He said: "See, my mom actually started working with this lady who works at [agency]. My mom also knows another lady who works at [local Arc], and I'm not sure who came up with it—I think that the job was through the lady [local Arc], I'm not sure. I've been a very busy man." These youths were aware of their mothers' efforts on their behalf, but it was rare for them, especially those with intellectual disabilities, to be aware of the full extent of their parents' investigative and planning efforts.

Gathering and making sense of transition-planning information is a form of care work, an emotional and practical effort that many parents make for their children. Parents of children and youths with disabilities do a wide range of care work, from home health care to tutoring (see Leiter 2004a, 2004b; Leiter et al. 2004). As children age, care work shifts from inside the home to schools and other domains (Wickham-Searl 1994). Transition planning is one more form of care-based labor. Mothers did the bulk of transition care work overall, although some fathers made significant contributions—this is consistent with other areas of care for children and youths with disabilities, in which mothers do much of the labor (Traustadóttir 2000). Like most care work, this transition-oriented care work is mostly invisible. Yet it has the potential to shape youths' opportunities in powerful ways. It makes parents key navigators, shaping their children's routes into adulthood. Parents often felt the burden of gathering information acutely—they were responsible but often felt that they lacked expertise.

Information was rarely readily available and had to be sought actively and individually by parents. In the words of one mother, Marka, "everybody's reinventing the wheel, over and over and over." Parents struggled to find information and several parents voiced their anxiety that they had missed crucial resources and thus had denied their children opportunities. Parents of college-bound youths were concerned about finding schools with good disability services that could meet their children's specific needs; "I think the thing that would be helpful from the colleges is more information," Nellie said. "They could have disabilities services. What does that mean? She doesn't need someone to tutor her on how to read. Is there someone there who she can meet to talk about issues? Or she can get a little confused on instructions. That's something I offer, a clarification—not that she wouldn't do it, but she might not understand or get the full depth of something. . . . So those kind of things are not clear. They may say, 'Oh, we have a support system.' Great. What does that mean?" In this instance, Nellie's daughter Rose had Asperger syndrome and Nellie was concerned about how colleges might support her daughter. Trisha, whose son Craig also has Asperger syndrome and wanted to attend an automotive vocational school, had a difficult time figuring out which programs would provide disability services and supports. "I just wish there was more transition stuff out there," she said. "More things to tell us where to look. We watch that Lincoln Tech commercial over and over again, and that might be something to look into, but that's only because they're advertising on TV. There's got to be somewhere out there that shows me and tells me what's out there."

Parents of youths with intellectual disabilities voiced their concerns about the potential pitfalls of missed information loudly and repeatedly. They felt tremendous uncertainty about the level and content of the services that the Department of Developmental Services (DDS) might provide to their children once they turned twenty-two and aged out of their entitlement to special education.[4] Ziggy explained: "I think that, having gone through having one kid going to college, people talk about the transition from high school to college and getting independent and all the rest of it. Folks have absolutely no idea, because if you have a kid that you know is not going to be independent, it changes everything. For my son [who went to college], it wasn't like we were casual about where he'd go to school. We gave him the attention, and we looked into it, and all the rest. . . . But we knew that he'd land on his feet no matter where he was. One way or another he'd land on his feet." In contrast, Ziggy anticipated that her daughter Yvonne would need ongoing employment and daily living supports into adulthood. Without these supports, she might end up at home with nothing to do all day, requiring Ziggy to quit her job so that she could stay home to ensure Yvonne's safety.

Parents also sought information from state agencies and organizations that provided state-funded adult services. Only three parents had contact with the Massachusetts Rehabilitation Commission (MRC), and only one had contact with a local Independent Living Center (ILC), both of which offer information about a broad range of disability resources and also provide some services. Most parents did not know that these organizations existed. In contrast, all parents of youths who would be eligible for Department of Developmental Services (DDS) services upon turning twenty-two were aware of DDS because high schools referred them to that agency. Out of the twenty-six parents whose children would be eligible for DDS services due to their intellectual disabilities, sixteen (62 percent) had contact with DDS in the year before our interviews. However, some parents voiced skepticism about the completeness of the information they had received from DDS.

ANGELA: We've had experiences from people in DDS before where they guided us wrong in terms of saying, "These are your best options," when there were many more options.

VALERIE: How do you think that happened?

ANGELA: Budget pressures are so difficult with state workers that sometimes the way they put things makes it sound as though you need to make choices or do certain things that you actually don't legally need to do. . . . It's not out-and-out blatant stuff, it's just discouragement or not opening up the full range of options, even when somebody is asking.

Many parents felt that public agencies could provide more information but sometimes would not disclose all the possible options. Leslie explained: "And I guess my feeling, too, is I've been in the system long enough. If you don't ask, they're not going to tell. You know?" This dynamic made parents worry that they were not asking the right questions and that their children might lose out as a result. Adam, who had a disability and worked in a community-based disability organization, explained that "they need to know that . . . these services are out here. There have been roads that are paved for you guys. You can walk, or you can continue to live in shadows or in the dark, totally unaware of what's going on in your community, what services are out there in your community for people like us, and what people out here get equipped, educated, and ready to help you with this transitional phase. Because it's just one part of your life. It's an important part of your life, what they call the 'rite of passage,' but it needs to be treated like that." Part of Adam's job, as he saw it, was to show youths and parents the road, but then they had to do the traveling themselves. Martha, a mother, also felt that parents needed to be proactive: "As I said, you have to kind of be out there. I got to knock on the door, no one's— I always tell people, no one's going to knock on your door unless you knock first, and phone calls, you know? There are some services out there, but unless you make the phone call, no one—I have never had anyone call."

In short, many parents felt that there was a kind of "if you don't ask, you're not told" policy. Although resources might exist, they were stealth resources.[5] Parents had to find the right agency, the right person, the right phone number to access them. Listening to parents talk about their search, it was as though they were describing an adventure video game like Myst, where you are in a maze and have to find and use clues that will eventually take you to the treasure. Nellie admitted: "You have to know the questions, and the questions are harder than the answers sometimes." Even those who found all the clues sometimes were unsure how to use them. Melinda felt overwhelmed by all the information she had amassed: "There's so much stuff out there to know. It really makes me nervous about all of the stuff I don't know, because this was *one Saturday* [devoted to a transition workshop], and I just felt like [*Sighs*]. What's going to bite me that I don't know about? So that's one of the scary things about the transition process, is that there's got to be a whole lot more out there that I should know about that I don't know about." Michelle felt much the same way when she was helping her daughter transition from high school: "I went to that training, but all it made me realize is how much we don't know. . . . It's just like, wow, there's so much. How am I supposed to internalize all of this and help my child?"

Even when schools and state agencies were forthcoming and helpful, parents rarely relied upon them solely for information. Maria, who did not have a computer, went to a local library to look up resources. Parents who were Internet savvy felt that the information available on the Internet was objective and reliable. Often they had relied upon it when their son or daughter received a diagnosis and they wanted to know the implications. As Jeffrey explained: "When we got the diagnosis, I went on the computer, I printed out everything on Asperger's and made copies for everyone in the family so that they could know what we've been dealing with and what the signs are and how to communicate. So I tried to educate them, because knowledge is power." Later on, when they were planning for life after high school, Jeffrey and other parents again used the Internet, although the range of Web-based resources could be overwhelming and challenging to navigate. A handful of parents became research experts in their quest for information, showing me binders and folders full of transition resources that rivaled those professionals in the field might have. Often, parents found local organizations that offered expertise.

Transition workshops conducted by community-based organizations were a key source of trusted information for most parents, with thirty-three of forty-nine families interviewed (67 percent) saying that they had attended at least one transition workshop. These organizations were often disability based, and the workshops ranged from several hours to several days, depending on the level of detail offered. Parents most often cited the Federation for Children with Special Needs (typically referred to as "the Federation") as a source of information; the Federation runs transition workshops throughout the year and across Massachusetts, in addition to providing Web-based and telephone support and holding an annual conference in Boston that is aimed primarily at parents. (Each state has at least one parent training and information center funded by the U.S. Department of Education. The Federation receives this funding and provides statewide support.)[6] The Asperger's Association of New England was a key resource for parents of youths with Asperger syndrome. For youths with intellectual disabilities, Mass Arc and some of the local Arcs ran transition workshops periodically. A few lawyers offered workshops that focused on guardianship and special needs trusts.

In addition to these disability-based organizations, a few ethnically based organizations offered workshops on special education rights, including transition, to the subpopulations they served, such as Haitian, Chinese, and Latino families. Maria, a Latino mother, said that she had attended a parent support group at Viva Urbana in Boston where parents shared information. In the case of organizations serving immigrants, meetings were held in the parents' native languages and in ways sensitive to families' cultural concerns. For example, the Boston Chinatown Neighborhood Association ran occasional parent workshops. Several African American parents who lived in Boston had attended workshops offered by Urban Pride, a community-based organization in Boston that works with urban families around special education issues (the other parent information center in the state funded by the U.S. Department of Education).

These community-based organizations helped by providing instrumental knowledge about youths' and parents' legal rights. They also provided access to other parents, which parents in this study cited as the best source of information—valid messengers, people who could be trusted to provide relevant information because of their lived expertise.[7] Norma, a professional whose daughter had a disability, stated baldly: "Everything I've learned, I've learned from another parent." One father, Peter, had a similar attitude: "Networking with other parents has always been number one." When asked what type of information would be useful to her, one mother, Marka, replied: "I would love to go to a parent group. There should be a road show, you know, like somebody like you that organizes it, and okay, this month we're going to do three sites throughout the state and it's all about—it's a panel of parents and—well, how did they do it? How did they build a house? How did they get the state thing, how did they keep control? Success stories on the road. And you know, somebody saying, 'Okay, I went through transitioning and these are the steps we did with the school.'" J.J. said that although the speakers his town's Special Education Parent Advisory Committee brought in were certainly valuable, "the most important thing I learned from a PAC is not the speakers. Yeah, we get speakers that'll teach you something, but it's learning where I stepped in the cow pies, so you don't step in the same cow pie that I did. And you learn, and I learned from the people who were ahead of me." There was often camaraderie among parents of youths with disabilities—a sense of belonging, particularly if their children had similar conditions—hearkening back to the origins of the parents' movement described in chapter 2. Parents sometimes became friends, and even if they did not, they were fellow travelers.

Parents did not view these exchanges as tit for tat, an exchange of one piece of information for another. Instead, parents shared the information broadly with each other, often paying forward, helping parents of younger children miss the cow pies they had experienced. This relationship is similar to the relationships that many parents have with other parents at their children's school, or parents they talk with on the sidelines of Saturday soccer or baseball games. Parents in those contexts may share information about summer camps, swimming lessons, or places to find babysitters. But there is a more intense insider dynamic among parents of children and youths with disabilities that is the result of shared experiences battling for health care, educational services, and other needed resources.

Parents often met through Special Education Parent Advisory Committee (SEPAC) meetings at their children's schools, or through organized activities such as Special Olympics. Sports events gave parents the chance to mingle informally and share information with each other while their children were engaged in sports practice or competitions. Marie found out about her son's middle school program from talking with another parent at a bowling league. Cassandra, who found out about her daughter's high school at a soccer game after searching on her own, said: "I truly believe God took care of me and led me to that soccer field that day, and that divine intervention, as I call it, really worked. And now Missy's got a real life, you know what I mean?" For parents who did not like joining groups, other parents were a crucial source of information. For instance, I asked Susan about workshops.

SUSAN: I can't stand any of that stuff. Hate it. I know, they have all kinds of programs.

VALERIE: They do.

SUSAN: Yes.

VALERIE: Yes, they do, and some people spend a lot of time going to those things.

SUSAN: No, I will tend to be friends with somebody who's gone to all of those things. [*Laughs.*]

Susan had a friend who attended many workshops and relied on her to find out which colleges had good reputations for working with students with learning disabilities, because their children had similar learning disabilities.

Parents who were fortunate enough to be in an informal network with an alpha parent—one with expertise about transition—benefited indirectly from those parents' expansive information networks. Alpha parents often worked in the disability field and therefore had access to both professional knowledge and resources and to the lived expertise of parenting a child with a disability. Almost all of these alpha parents were mothers; although several fathers such as Jeffrey and J.J. did a great deal of searching and navigation work, mothers did the bulk of it. It is largely gendered, like other forms of care work (see Meyer 2000 for a detailed analysis).

Peter and Ann were grateful to a mother they knew from Special Olympics who was a parent and a disability professional—she was the first person to talk with them about guardianship and Supplemental Security Income (SSI) benefits. While their daughters were doing gymnastics, all the parents would sit together in the waiting room and chat, and the alpha mother would sometimes dole out information and advice. "I don't want to share her with anyone," Peter half-joked, recognizing that this mother clued them in to resources that other parents had not found on their own. Likewise, Celie, whose son had a physical disability, mentioned an alpha parent in her personal network who worked in the disability field: "I have a friend who has a son that's a little bit older than Frankie, so she's kind of going down the road before me. So that helps a lot of have someone that's been through it a little bit. . . . I didn't have the expectations, too, prior to meeting her and her son that I have now. Like Frankie's going to go—he got his learner's permit on his birthday, and he's going for a driving eval[uation] in October, and I don't know how it's going to happen, but supposedly they think maybe he can drive a car." Information from alpha parents can have ripple effects, as word of opportunities moves through the grapevine. Rita, another mother I interviewed, happened to meet Celie several months later at an annual Federation meeting and learned that Frankie had gotten his driving license. No one had told her that her son Steve might be able to drive using hand controls, and she was excited to pursue it.

Occasionally, parents who were not working in the disability field became alpha parents by putting so much time and effort into conducting independent research into transition resources and opportunities for their children that this care work became a part-time job. Janet was among them. "I'll be honest with you, Valerie," she said. "I'm just like a researcher. I'm a researcher. . . . I should have gone to law school and done contract law, that was my thing. But I'm doing it here unofficially." Janet had piles of carefully organized files packed with information in her dining room—a file on federal legislation related to access to vocational education, another on person-centered planning processes in Minnesota. This was not a run-of-the-mill Internet search—Janet had read and synthesized these materials as she searched for resources for her daughter's future. As a result of her impressive research abilities, other parents had started to rely upon her expertise and her status had risen accordingly—she had recently been elected to a leadership position in her local SEPAC.

As helpful as these exchanges could be, there were some limits to the camaraderie among parents of youths with intellectual disabilities. Parents whose children were approaching the end of their entitlement to a publicly funded education at age twenty-two occasionally worried about sharing too much information with other parents if they had managed to negotiate a good set of services for their child with the state agency (DDS) that provides adult services. Because the demand for these services outstripped the supply, parents gradually became aware that their children were competing with other youths for them. These parents saw a zero-sum game: if one youth got a service, that might mean others would not receive any services or a lower level of services. Jean and Dirk, whose daughter had an intellectual disability, related a long story about two families they knew, in which one young woman had gotten a placement in a group home only to lose it because word got out through the grapevine. Another mother whose child was waiting for residential placement called DDS and the agency that ran the group home to complain and ask why her daughter did not also have a placement. As a result, the young woman who had the placement lost her housing and had to stay at home, and the other family did not benefit as a result of that loss. Such cautionary tales could make parents wary of sharing good news about DDS services with other families, reducing the exchange of information between parents who were now competitors for scarce resources. With the exception of these later occasional tensions, parents largely saw other parents of youths with disabilities as crucial and trustworthy sources of information.

Professional Sources of Social Capital

Schools were an important source of social capital, but the amount of information shared by schools was uneven. Both youths and parents gathered information from schools directly. Teachers were a key source of social capital for youths directly—36 percent of youths mentioned talking with their teachers about the future. Teachers had the potential to become important mentors because youths came into daily contact with them over the course of a year or more. Craig, who was being mentored by a computer teacher, was the only student allowed to help fix the computers—he and the teacher worked together to set up blocks on the computers so that students could not download viruses, and to fix the computers when viruses did get through. A teacher who was mentoring Missy through the transition-planning process at her school, had asked Missy about what she wanted to do after leaving her high school, urging her to think about her goals before her upcoming transition-planning meeting. Missy said: "Well, she was like, 'What do you want to do *at* [school], and then what do you want to do when you *leave* [school]?' She was like, 'Let's start with the future outside of [school] and then the future inside of [school].'" This teacher helped Missy prepare for her transition planning meetings at her school by pushing her to think through how what she was doing in high school supported her post–high school goals. Other school professionals were also sources of support and advice for one-third of the youths, including special education liaisons and aides or principals.

Guidance counselors played a much smaller role than one might expect. Although youths did work sometimes with them on social and emotional issues in a more therapeutic context, a minority, just 23 percent, said that they had talked with their guidance counselors about their future after high school during the previous year. A few youths in public schools mentioned that their guidance counselors worked with large numbers of students, which could make it difficult to get individualized attention. Rose, who had Asperger syndrome and was gearing up for her college search in the fall of her junior year, had a new guidance counselor because her counselor last year had retired. The new counselor had so many students that she was meeting them in groups, which made Rose worry that she would not be able to get a strong letter of recommendation for college because the counselor did not know her. Frankie could not count on much assistance from his guidance counselor at school either: "Not to badmouth my school in any way, but the guidance counselors aren't the best. They don't help the kids get into school or anything. Like when my sister went, she, like, had—she had to tell the guidance counselor what she was doing to get ready for college. And the guidance counselor said, 'Well, okay.'" Even if youths could get attention, guidance counselors in public schools did not always have specific knowledge about which colleges were the best fit for youths with particular types of disabilities, in terms of the accommodations and supports provided.

In contrast, the college-bound students at private schools reported receiving much more intensive college counseling. The private schools were much smaller than the public schools, all of them specialized in educating youths with disabilities, and college entry was part of their focus. It was important for them to show their effectiveness by documenting successful college placement rates. Several of the private schools had annual college fairs and distributed lists of colleges and universities the schools' alumnae attended after graduation. Anna and Frederick, who attended different schools, each took a transition class in which they received guidance about applying to college and worked on their personal essays. Frederick's school prided itself on its college placement rates—it was a major selling point for the school. In his junior year, Frederick had already visited several colleges through field trips arranged by the school. "But I'm not saying that I necessarily have to go to any of the colleges pre-scribed there," he said. "But I think it's good to go through the process of visiting to really get any degree of what makes a college right for me, rather than a college in and of itself being good." The goal of the visits was to help the students figure out what they wanted in a college, what would fit them best. Joseph, whose private school specializes in learning disabilities, met with his guidance counselor once every week or two and had developed a list of colleges to explore. He said that his school started college prepara-tion "really early." In his senior year, Joseph said, he would meet with his guidance counselor once a week. His mother, Ursula, explained: "The one thing they do that I think is good is, they definitely try to put the kids in the right colleges. Sometimes I think they are too—how did Joseph and I describe this? Not easy, but they have a list that they say, these are the schools that our kids would do well at. Obviously they want their kids to succeed in college, but I've noticed kids are branching out and trying to get off of that list, but also go to schools that have learning centers." Youths at private schools who were college bound received more specialized coun-seling and more information about and connections with colleges and universities that provided good supports for students with disabilities. Those youths felt as though they had a handle on the application process and the services they could expect from colleges.

A sizeable minority of youths (23 percent) did not report talking with any adults at their schools during the past year around transition issues. They relied primarily upon their parents as sources of support and infor-mation. Very few were aware that they could seek information and support on their own from sources outside their schools. Three who were fortunate to discover disability organizations whose staff specialized in transition issues relied on those organizations rather than their schools. Mika, who had a physical disability, relied upon staff at Easter Seals of Massachusetts and at the Massachusetts Rehabilitation Commission (MRC) for information about negotiating eligibility and rules for adult services. She said: "Easter Seals introduced me to a lot, so I found out about voc[ational] rehab[ilitation] and things like that because you know the laws have changed on the loan companies so they make it more difficult for people like me who are like, 'What's voc rehab,' you know? So I'm glad that I found [Easter Seals and MRC staff] and say, 'Where do I go?' and they usually point me in the right directions." Darren received advice from both Easter Seals and the Massachusetts Commission for the Blind, which helped him start college and find a job after finishing high school. Justin received counseling and resources only from MRC in the form of mentoring, advice about college, and tuition support.

Social capital could also flow indirectly from schools to youths, with parents as intermediaries. Parents were much more likely than youths to discuss future plans with school staff—forty out of forty-nine parents (82 percent) interviewed mentioned at least one school staff member (and often several) when asked whom they had talked with about their child's future in the past year.[8] In particular, parents relied on teachers (47 percent), guidance counselors (37 percent), and other school professionals (63 percent) such as therapists, special education directors, and special education liaisons (for youths who had been placed outside their school districts). Half of all parents had talked with multiple staff members at their children's schools. For example, Ann mentioned a speech therapist who spoke as an advocate on behalf of her daughter Sarah: "At the meeting she would always speak up. If she saw we were stumped, she would stand up at the meeting and say, 'Look, this is not my area, I'm speech, but this is what you need to do, because you're looking at her becoming an adult taking care of herself.' So even though it wasn't in her realm, she had a lot of experience. She's retired now. She had a lot of experience and she really was interested in seeing her have good outcomes." While schools were an important source of information, many parents were unwilling to rely upon them entirely. Not all schools were equally forthcoming.

Parents' understanding of schools' reticence to share information varied. Parents who were more generous stated that the schools simply did not seem to know about all the resources out there. Parents who were less generous, and some professionals, thought that it was the schools' job to have that information and share it. Roseanne, a mother, explained that "the schools, they don't come out and tell you because they don't want to offer too much because then [they] have to pay for it. They don't want to give you too much information because then you're dangerous." Norma, a professional, added: "It's not necessarily a lie or something they're doing wrong, but they haven't informed you, and you as a parent want them to just do their job. You have an expectation when you go into a school, the people who are providing that service know how to do their job. So there is no excuse for them not knowing." She felt that it was the schools' job to gather transition information and share it with youths and parents. Janet, whose daughter had autism, felt that the schools were not as accountable for youths with disabilities who were not college bound as they were for college-bound youths: "The teachers don't even know about what, you know, placements and stuff like that are out there and they're not sup- posed to really tell, or whatever. You know what I mean? But you've got to get off your butt and realize. You're talking about an investment in a child's education? Come on. If you know that Suzie is on that track, you know what? There should be a next step to take her to the next level. And if this school placement is the type to continue that, then there you go. And they had a kid for three years, and if you know, okay, she's really good at technical stuff, then they should know." According to the youths, parents, and professionals interviewed, schools do contribute some important transition information and opportunities, but the level of trans- mission is uneven. Youths and parents who relied on schools as their sole source of social capital could miss important information about opportunities and resources.

Unequal Amounts of Direction

Youths and their parents journeyed through this maze of information, with parents spending varying amounts of time creating social capital for their children. Youths and their families had to create their own maps into the future, seeking out information from a variety of sources to meet their spe- cific needs and projected journeys. Jane, whose daughter turned twenty- two and transitioned from high school the week before our interview, noted: "I think I've learned that through the years. It's like, don't take anybody's word of saying, 'This is all that can be done,' or 'This is the way it has to be.' That, you know, you have to—you know, either dig a little further or figure out, Well, I'll go around another way to get what I need." She went on to describe some parents who did not take such an active role. "It is unfortunate for a lot of the families who don't know anything or who are sitting waiting for someone to tell them. And I hear that all the time, kids who are eighteen and parents saying, 'Well, you know, what's the next program the school's gonna send them to?' or 'Where are they gonna go as an adult?' And they're waiting, honestly, for the school to make this great recommendation to this other program. And when they hear, like, there's nothing, there's no entitlement, you're done, it's really scary. It's, like, 'Oh, what am I supposed to do? I have to go to work.' Yeah, this is the way it is. You know? It's difficult."

A few parents who expended a great deal of effort seeking information were more direct in their criticism of parents who did less and sometimes attempted to cajole less active parents into taking a stronger advocacy role.

RACHEL: So it's worrisome. It's worrisome to see that none of this stuff is offered to people. You know, they should be able to have a life, just like anybody else. But if they don't have a voice, if they don't have a parent that wants that for them? . . . I'm working with [other parents], they're a little resistant right now because I think—I sometimes feel like they're judging what I'm doing. They don't want to be as involved as I am. They love their kid, not any different, but their involvement . . .

VALERIE: What you're doing is a fair amount of work.

RACHEL: It's a lot of work. And they don't want that work. I don't mind that work right now, because I feel like after what I just went through, it's giving him a life and so I get the benefits of it. You know what I mean?

Likewise, Ursula was concerned about parents who did not advocate for their children as strongly as she did.

URSULA: I'm sure there are a lot of kids there who are in that boat, who really are struggling. Their parents aren't as interested or don't—

VALERIE: Or don't know.

Ursula: Don't know. Some parents, I don't think, care as much. All parents care. Don't know, or don't know what to do, or don't know what resources are out there, or don't know how to approach the problem. I felt like my legal background actually came in really helpful.

Well-educated parents were more easily able to engage in the search for information than were others. Both Ursula and Rachel were educated, upper-middle-class women. Rachel was not working outside the home, and Ursula had an advanced degree. They each had personal resources upon which they could draw when advocating for their children. Both struggled with the idea that not all parents advocated as strongly as they did. Martha, another mother, felt so strongly that all parents must advocate that she took it upon herself to pester other parents into action: "Again, if you have any information from other parents or if they need—I'm always, I'm always actually always throwing information and sometimes I think parents are like, 'Just shut up, I don't want to hear it right now.' But I say, 'But you have to do this. Can't wait, you have to do it now.'"

These mothers were voicing an expectation that all parents, but especially "good" parents, will advocate for their children. This expectation adds another component to parents' jobs as parents—an advocacy imperative.[9] The flip side of this logic is that if parents do not garner social capital and use it effectively, their children will suffer the consequences. Inactive parents are framed as "bad" parents. In Cassandra's case, other parents' inaction demonstrated to her that she must advocate for her daughter: "I happened to be at a softball field watching a special needs soccer game, saw someone that used to go to the school years ago whose child is now twenty-six. And they didn't advocate like I did. And their child sits home four days a week and goes and volunteers somewhere one day a week, right. So completely what I do not want my child to do. I want her to have a meaning to life." This advocacy imperative does not simply place responsibility for action upon parents. The moral framing is quite powerful here—parents, not disability policies and service systems, are blamed if their children get fewer resources than other children as a result of inaction.

A few proactive parents were savvy about social factors that could make it difficult for other parents to fulfill this advocacy imperative. These parents acknowledged that many parents faced barriers to advocacy, namely, poverty, single parenthood, substantial time spent in paid work, having English as a second language, and low educational levels. Professionals were the most understanding and least judgmental of inactive parents, because they worked with a wider range of youths and families and had a broader view of the transition process. Scott, who worked with immigrant families, highlighted some of the cultural barriers that immigrant parents sometimes experienced: "I think a lot of parents, they do see schools and teachers as authoritative figures and they're formidable and you have to be scared about them, you have to respect them. Do not challenge them, all they say is right. But we're teaching them something different. They're not always right. . . . I mean, it's immigration. I mean, immigration means you go into a totally different culture, and I think some parents realize that if they don't speak up, there'll be nothing." Amanda, a professional who was an immigrant parent of an adult with an intellectual disability, was most understanding in her assessment of less active parents in general, not just immigrants. Her goal was "helping parents to know what to do. There is no parent voluntarily decided, 'I'm not going to help my child.' This is not part of being a parent. Parents love their child any way possible, but they will do whatever necessary to help that child. And you find when you are not educated, how are you going to find your way?"

Inequalities in knowledge existed in conjunction with parents' educational levels—parents with more education were better equipped to engage with schools and service systems in terms of understanding their children's rights and to use that knowledge to put pressure on systems. Inequalities also existed according to immigration status—immigrant parents whose cultures stressed deference to people in authority were less likely to ask questions and advocate. Three professionals, Amanda, Scott, and Adam, stated specifically that parents whose cultures stigmatized disability were less likely to come forward to request information and advocate for their children. Having a child with a disability could be a source of shame. In some cultures childhood disability is a strong signal about the family, for example, a punishment for misconduct by the child's ancestors.[10] Immigrants and refugees who came from countries with repressive regimes were much less likely to advocate for their children because they feared reprisal from the government if they spoke up. When I asked Bernie, a professional, about the role that culture played in working with families, he mentioned Cambodian families in particular: "We haven't done a real good job with that population. I think we're dealing with a lot of the adults, are, you know, refugees from the Pol Pot era and—their experience with government is certainly not—we may not get past that."

Immigrant and refugee parents sometimes feared that the Department of Social Services (DSS) would take their children away from them if they pushed too hard for services. The names of the Department of Developmental Services (DDS), which provided services to adults with intellectual disabilities, and the Department of Social Services (DSS), the state's child welfare agency, were unfortunately all too alike. This contributed to parents' confusion about which state agency might help their child and which might take her or him away. It was difficult to counter these strongly held fears and confusions—why should families trust complete strangers who work for the government, if their experiences with government workers had been oppressive in their countries of origin? Amanda recounted a story about one Haitian family she worked with where she did ultimately succeed. She visited in person repeatedly, but they would not answer their door. Sometimes she would see them peeking at her from behind their curtains, but they were too frightened to open the door. Finally, after six months, they let her in. The family eventually came to see her as an extended family member, but it took a tremendous amount of effort on her part to make that happen. Professionals with large caseloads or limited experience working with immigrants from other cultures might not be able to break down those barriers or might come to view families as disinterested in their children's services.

Youths had unequal amounts of social capital from their families and schools—schools and families differed in terms of the amount of social capital they collected and bestowed upon youths to help them find their way in life after high school. These inequalities became evident as I examined the information that youths and parents gathered and used to help youths achieve their goals.

Making Their Own Maps

Youths make their own maps, with their parents' help, in their quest to plan out their journeys into adulthood. They relied on their parents and professionals at their schools for support and information, only rarely encountering resources through community-based disability organizations that could have helped them. Parents relied on a wider range of resources, including school professionals, professionals in state disability agencies, the Internet, community-based organizations, and especially other parents of youths with disabilities. Social relations between youths and their parents, and between parents and outside organizations, created crucial conduits for resources. Parents rarely stopped and asked just one person for directions along the journey—they asked multiple people and then pieced together that information to sketch out possible routes that youths could take into the future. Fellow travelers—other parents of youths with disabilities—were seen as especially trustworthy sources of information. Schools were just one source of social capital out of many, providing less information about transition than many youths, parents, and professionals thought they ought to. The more embedded parents were in disability-focused social structures, such as parent groups and disability organizations, the more they were able to draw on informal sources of social capital to help find their way.

This map-making enterprise puts substantial responsibility upon youths and their families to collect information, make sense of it, and then use it. Parents in particular are responsible for this care work, and other parents were often judgmental if they did not engage in it with gusto. Michelle, a professional, described the process of gathering transition information as "a very middle-class model. You've got the information, so self-help. Self-determination. You take this information and run with it." Not all parents were engaged with systems of information or were equipped to "run with it" if they did get access to information. Having exceptional parents is one factor that may help in youths' transition. "However, not everyone can have exceptional parents" (Pascall and Hendey 2004, 165).[11] Social capital, therefore, was distributed unequally among families of youths with disabilities. Just as social class has been found to shape children's educational experiences (Lareau 2000), here parental education and immigration status shaped the level of information gathered and used by parents of youths with disabilities.

Power is embedded in knowledge, and having knowledge made parents feel that they and their children had some control over their destinies. Leslie, whose son Damien had Asperger syndrome, told me: "To me, knowledge is power." Tee-Tee, whose son Eddy had just started attending a day program for adults with intellectual disabilities, shared a similar sentiment: "See, knowledge is a powerful thing." For Tee-Tee, knowledge gave her the ability to choose a day program that she felt took good care of her son. For Leslie, it was a matter of finding a good vocational school and getting support to help her son be successful. Knowledge contributes to youths' and parents' capacity to make informed decisions. It does not necessarily make people take action, but parents believed that knowledge was crucial in opening up opportunities for their children.

Youths were not guaranteed to arrive at the destinations they desired—none of us have that guarantee. But the youths had a sense of where they wanted to go, and they and their parents strove to find routes and resources that could help them along on their journeys. Those efforts did matter—the youths whose families had garnered more social capital had developed more detailed routes to their desired destinations. It is also important to note that social capital was distributed unevenly within families as well as between them, with parents holding more social capital than their children. Youths may have determined their desires, but parents did the bulk of the work of identifying routes and resources to achieve those goals.

From youths' perspectives, this inequality in knowledge between themselves and their parents was not a problem. In fact, they were counting on their parents to gather information and resources on their behalf. When we asked if they needed additional information to achieve their goals after high school, most said no. (It was largely parents who had niggling worries about the information that they should have discovered but had not.) Carl responded: "I don't think so. I can get whatever I need from my school and I can get—my mom will help me as much as she can." A handful of students wanted information about colleges, but much of that information had to be gathered through personal experience. Joseph felt that "colleges send you a fair amount when you request information, but I think you have to go and actually see the learning center that they have." Rose thought that she "would love to stay overnight at a college, maybe not around now, but sometime." Mika's request for information was more specific—were there any college scholarships specifically for students with disabilities? (There was in fact a scholarship program for students with disabilities through United Cerebral Palsy.) Likewise, a few students had precise questions about preparing for their future careers, questions that would be answered through experience. Frederick said he would "definitely like to know more about what would be the proper channels to express—to submit potential articles [about video games]." A few youths were more philosophical in their quest for information. Hermione, who was starting college the following weekend, said: "Well, I mean I guess there's probably a lot I don't know that I'll learn along the way." And Damien said "there might be [questions] in the future, but right now I don't really know what it is, like it'll be unveiled or something." They had the information they needed for now and acknowledged that they needed more life experience before they could pose additional questions.

5

College, Rights, and Goodness of Fit

College is a well-traveled pathway between adolescence and adulthood. Over the past fifty years, more and more youths have entered college—as of 2006, 66 percent of recent high school completers did so (NCES 2008). Like their peers, youths with disabilities are increasingly likely to enroll in postsecondary education: their number rose by 17 percent between 1987 and 2003 (Wagner et al. 2005). Almost one in ten undergraduates currently report having a disability or a chronic condition.[1] Some of the rise in postsecondary participation among youths with disabilities may be attributed to disability civil rights legislation, namely Section 504 of the Rehabilitation Act and the Americans with Disabilities Act (ADA), which prohibit discrimination against people with disabilities and require postsecondary institutions to provide adaptations and accommodations to students with disabilities. Section 504 and the ADA enhance the perception that youths with disabilities can continue their studies after high school, that college is a viable option. Disability rights can influence the self-perceptions of individuals with disabilities by guaranteeing nondiscriminatory treatment and reasonable accommodations. They can also create cultural shifts, transforming the way that others perceive and treat individuals with disabilities (see Engel and Munger 2003).

Even though legislation has increased educational opportunities for youths with disabilities, its implementation may be uneven, reducing its impact. Some of this unevenness may result from colleges' practices.[2] Youths and parents become aware that some colleges are more disability friendly than others and look for clues as to which schools will provide the best supports and accessibility. Youths' patchy use of their rights can also contribute to some of the unevenness in the implementation of these laws.

Two kinds of fit came into play in this search for the right colleges and the role that disability rights play in the search. First, youths tried to find the college that best fit them based on social environment, academic offerings, distance from home, opportunities to play on sports teams, and other considerations, including disability services. Second, youths expressed reluctance to use disability rights in college. Disability rights did not always fit them well as individuals, for multiple reasons.

Finding a College That Fits

College expectations were nearly universal among youths with physical, sensory, and learning disabilities and did not vary by social class or gender—youths understood that a college education was necessary for them to achieve their career and life goals. The vast majority of youths with physical, sensory, and hidden disabilities planned to attend college immediately after high school (23 of the 26, or 88 percent). What going to college meant to the youths varied, however, from taking a few courses online or at a local community college to studying full-time at a nearby state university while living at home or attending a college or university at a distance from home and living in a dorm.

High school students typically take into consideration a wide range of characteristics when searching for the right college. The first consideration among the youths interviewed was whether a college could support their proposed area of study, which included theater, engineering, architecture, English, biochemistry, Judaic studies, psychology, veterinary care, and writing. College and career goals often arose from life experiences. Anna loved animals, for example, and had done volunteer work caring for them. She knew that she wanted to be a veterinary technician, so she searched for colleges that had specific programs that would prepare her for that field. Katherine wanted to be a writer. She aspired to write a novel about her life and wrote songs in her free time. Emily also enjoyed writing. She wanted to go to college to study theater to become an acting teacher, "but it's not the most money-bringing-in kind of a job. So I might do like nutritionist stuff as well, like to have something to fall back on." Emily was writing a book on nutrition at the time. "It's still a work in progress, but it's there . . . it's humorous. So it's like one of my chapters is 'The Evils of the Hershey Kiss,' and 'Why We Love Fat,' and stuff like that." Emily, like several other youths, felt she needed to have a fallback plan in college because her preferred career goal was unlikely to provide much income.

There was a hard-core group of young men with learning disabilities and Asperger syndrome who wanted to get into the video-gaming industry. Carl, who had a learning disability, saw himself as an expert of sorts: "In order to really understand video games, you almost have to be addicted to them in some way or another. . . . You kind of have to have almost that outer world reconnect, otherworldly connection." Coleman wanted to work on the design aspect of gaming but understood that he would need to study some computer science to get there. Frederick, who had Asperger syndrome, saw himself as a game reviewer and had already started writing reviews: "I've actually got a spotless track record of having submitted an article for at least every issue of the monthly school paper throughout the entire year. Each and every one of them, of course, being video game reviews—or at least game related. Hey—that's my shtick, yeah. . . . Let's just say that I've had experiences with games, akin to the sort of emotional gravitas you'd expect from a legitimately immaculate cinematic achievement like, say, *The Godfather*." Frederick made it clear that he was not simply a "fan boy" but someone capable of writing critical reviews of new games, and was taking all honors classes to prepare him for college.

Teddy and Justin both chose their prospective careers based on their experiences of living with a disability. Teddy, who had Asperger syndrome and had seen several psychologists over the years, had recently decided that he wanted to study psychology: "When I was younger, I wanted to do a lot of computer stuff. Now I really, in the last six months to a year, am really interested in mental health." His goal was to become a residential counselor. Justin also wanted to study psychology so that he could work with youths with disabilities, as the result of poor experiences with counselors: "I want to do psychology, because I want to—even in [town] when I went to a psychologist—I saw a counselor, a psychologist, I don't know what he was, but he's like, 'I couldn't really connect with you because I didn't really know what it was like to be in a wheelchair.' So I want to be that one person that can say, 'Listen, I know what it's like. I know what it's like to have somebody help you do this and help you do that.' They gave me a guy who's new, and he's like, 'I have no idea what it's like to be you. It must be horrible.' I'm like, 'Yeah, it is! Why do you think I'm here talking with you? Thanks, buddy.'" Justin's goal was to be there for the next generation of youths like himself, and college was the means to that goal.

Like other high school students, these young people also took into consideration colleges' proximity to home, class sizes, opportunities to participate in sports and other activities, and, of course, the cost of tuition and the availability of financial aid. Disability-related issues were just one more factor on a long list that they considered when deciding which colleges fit them best.

Parents were much more concerned than their children were about the provision of disability services on campuses—it was primarily parents who pushed for information on that topic. Getting information about what it is like to be a student with a particular disability on a particular campus can be tricky, however. Although all colleges must comply with Section 504 and the ADA, youths experienced challenges obtaining information about colleges' disability accommodations and services. Details about programs of study, class sizes, and so forth are published in guides to colleges and often included in print and Web-based marketing materials created by colleges—these are selling points. But information about disability services is not typically highlighted in the same way. Youths and parents had to search out that information through published sources, social connections, visits to campuses, and conversations with college disability services staff.

When possible, they gathered information from the few published college guides that focus specifically on students with learning disabilities or attention deficit disorders (see, e.g., Kravitz and Wax 2001; Mangrum and Strichart 1997). These guides provide some helpful clues about which schools might provide good supports but are not always up to date. Joseph, who had a learning disability and wanted to study engineering or architecture, said that he wanted to attend a college with a writing center, as writing was the most challenging area for him academically. He felt that "you have to go and actually see the learning center that they have to be able to determine what they have." He and his mother, Ursula, were researching schools using a published guide on colleges that were rated highest for students with learning disabilities. Ursula explained the way the guide worked: "They break it down. Four-year structured programs, four-year self-directed, two-year structured, two-year self-directed. Joseph is definitely focused on the self-directed programs, but he's very aware. He said, 'I definitely need a writing center.' He said, 'I cannot go to a college without a writing center.'"

Yet college guides do not cover all disabilities—youths with less prevalent disabilities, including physical and sensory disabilities and Asperger syndrome, had to rely more on sources of social capital for information, resources produced by parents and youths through their relations within formal and informal structures. These included other parents, disability organizations, and private high schools. Rose, a public high school junior with Asperger syndrome, said that "the Asperger Association does have a list of colleges where people have done well."

Students at private high schools relied mainly on their schools for information. These schools prided themselves on their college placement rates, so it was in their interest to keep those rates high. Several had college resource rooms and guidance counselors who worked intensively with students to help them with the college application process. Trevor, a junior with Asperger syndrome, was taking a college prep class in which his teacher brought in pictures of college campuses and explained the kinds of questions students should ask when they went on visits. Frederick, also a junior with Asperger syndrome, explained that his private school focused explicitly on college planning in its curriculum: "They're very dedicated to the college-planning process. And they're just taking us to a bunch of local colleges. In fact, my teacher is actually a night teacher at [a college] . . . so he has more than enough experience to provide the tools we need. In fact, that aforementioned college-planning elective is actually mandatory for juniors and seniors. And, hey, I'll gladly do it." Frederick's college prep class went even further than the search and application process, including material on dorm skills to help students adjust to living on campus once they arrived at college.

All the youths at private schools said that their schools provided them with information about which colleges had accepted alumni from their school. Elyse, whose son Coleman had a learning disability, described how her son's school "did a huge presentation about all of the different kinds of levels of services at colleges and trying to highlight, 'Here's a huge amount of services, here's just a little bit of services, and there's all this stuff in the middle.' And talking about how some of the kids from [the school] have transitioned to different places and the different kinds of success stories I guess is what we were hearing." Several students mentioned that colleges had visited their schools, clearly inviting students to apply. Roseanne, whose daughter Anna had a learning disability, was grateful for the assistance that Anna's school provided regarding the processes of applying to colleges and writing college application essays.

Students at public schools did not have these kinds of rich social resources. Several mentioned that their guidance counselors worked with large numbers of students, which could make it difficult to get individualized attention and advice, as noted earlier. The private schools were much smaller than the public schools, all of them specialized in educating youths with disabilities, and all had created relationships with colleges that welcomed their students. These resources helped youths and parents sort out which colleges might provide good disability services. Yet this emphasis on college placement rates among private schools could have a down side. Grace, a junior with a learning disability, complained that at her school, "a lot of kids don't go to very good colleges. . . . I don't even know if they want to, but I feel that they do have the potential to do better." Grace felt students were guided to colleges that would accept them but that might not be particularly competitive, to keep her school's college placement rate high.

Once students and parents had gathered initial information about potential schools, they could begin to figure out which could meet the students' particular needs. Their needs related to their disabilities were often very specific. Carl, for instance, who had a learning disability, wanted books on tape because he read so slowly. Coleman needed "a little bit more time" on tests because of his learning disability, as did Anna; both had learning disabilities. Kaiser, who had Asperger syndrome, needed extended time on research projects and sometimes used a scribe in classes. Rose, who also had Asperger syndrome, just needed a little help deciphering teachers' instructions on assignments. Both Frankie and

Steve had physical disabilities and needed accessible dorm rooms that could accommodate their wheelchairs, and classrooms in physically accessible buildings. Steve had already decided that one nearby college was not an option for him, because "it wouldn't be a place where I could get around by myself, because that place is really old. And so I'd have to know that that place would be like relatively new, so that it will be easy for me to get around." Several state colleges and universities were widely perceived as physically accessible. Rita, Steve's mother, said: "I've heard about [a state college], just from physical therapists and teachers have said they've known students that were physically challenged and went to [the state college]. That's the only school—and Steve has been down there."[3]

College visits were the next step in assessing whether a school met a youth's intellectual, social, and disability needs. Several youths started their visits earlier than their school peers to allow more time to assess the goodness of fit. Rose had started college shopping in the summer before her junior year. After those visits, she explained: "I'm really interested in Mount Holyoke because they seem really friendly. Other places I kind of like are University of New Hampshire and Connecticut College. Basically, I'm looking for something closish to home, though if it's close to New York City and I can take the train, that is very fine with me, so I'm also planning on visiting maybe a few New York colleges." Frankie began his college visits early in the fall of his junior year. His mother, Celie, said: "We looked at [private colleges], and I think this Saturday we're going to go to [state college], and then there's a bunch of open houses at other state schools this fall. Even though he's only a junior, like for my daughter we didn't start looking until probably like the summer before senior year, but for Frankie, because it's going to take a lot more to get a right fit, we're starting early."

During their campus visits, youths and parents looked for signals that students with disabilities were welcome. Anna had visited two colleges that had good programs for the major she wanted to pursue: "Well, I applied to—I went to [one college] and I knew I didn't want to go there because my mom noticed that they don't have a lot of disability services. They don't even have a ramp for people with wheelchairs. And then I just applied to one in Vermont and [my current college]. I didn't want to go too far away, so that's how I made my decision." Even though Anna had a learning disability, not a physical disability, she and her mother interpreted the lack of ramps on one college's campus as a signal that the college did not accept and welcome students with disabilities and decided that it would not be receptive to her needs. Frederick described his positive feelings after a recent visit to a college in Boston: "We didn't get a chance to [meet with disability services staff] because all the information sessions were booked up. It was just a general tour. But even when I was there, I could really feel this very homecoming vibe that they were going to be very accepting." In fact, the college that Frederick had visited has specialized services for students with Asperger syndrome and strong experience working with them. Even though he was not able to get information about specific services during his visit, he liked the way that he was treated while on campus. The disability services website for this college was also lively and welcoming, another positive signal to prospective students with disabilities. Frederick's mother had followed up with the disability services staff at the college and investigated the specific services provided by the school, and the family was considering it seriously.

In addition to these subjective assessments, youths and parents relied on several objective indicators when assessing the goodness of fit. The ratio of disability services staff to students was a key indicator of the level of attention students might expect to receive. Youths and parents also wanted to know that the staff had experience with a particular disability, an issue especially for those with Asperger syndrome. Not as many colleges had experience working with students on the autism spectrum, because the increase in youths diagnosed with those conditions was fairly recent. Nellie, whose daughter has Asperger syndrome, explained that "the high school had a list of colleges last April and they asked different schools that have disability services. But I have no idea what that means to that institution. And this population is very different from, say, the Down syndrome population or the dyslexic population or the ADHD population." Although colleges might know how to provide solid accommodations for students with learning disabilities or ADHD, much more prevalent conditions, it was not clear that they would understand her daughter's needs.

The size of the college and class size were important indicators too. Parents thought that their children would receive more attention at smaller colleges with smaller class sizes, where they would be less likely to fall between the cracks. Roberta, whose daughter Hermione has Asperger syndrome and would start college the week after we talked, had some concerns: "So I'm also concerned about how big and spread out it is. But the fact that she's in this small program—these twenty-four kids live together, take classes together. So it's like a little school-within-a-school kind of thing." The smaller size of the program made it unlikely that no one would notice if Hermione ran into any difficulties.

The only way for some youths and parents to learn more about the likely scope of adaptations and supports was to ask the disability services staff on campus directly. Celie complained that she had "been calling the state schools that are having Saturday or Sunday open houses, and I call the disability office. I'm like, 'Are you going to be there for the open house?' And they're like, 'No, we work Monday to Friday.' It's like, all right, that stinks, because we're going to look at the school, but then we're going to have to come back and talk to you guys separately. It's not like it's easy or cut and dried." Information about academic programs, life on the residence campus, and so on was available at the open houses, but information about disability services typically was not. This meant that youths and parents could not take advantage of those relatively anonymous events to ask questions about disability-related issues. Instead, they had to initiate one-on-one conversations with disability services staff separately. Some parents worried about disclosing information about a disability in advance of the college's application decision, fearing that it might hurt their child's chances of being accepted, even though federal law prohibits discrimination on the basis of disability.

When Rights Don't Fit

What youths and parents alike typically did not understand was that students enter a new world of adult disability rights when they leave high school and enter college. Parental rights vanish once their children enter college—youths are then considered adults and are expected to advocate for themselves using their rights under the ADA or Section 504. Also, while high schools are responsible for identifying and assessing potential students with disabilities under IDEA, Section 504, and the ADA, college students must identify themselves to their college's disability services office, take responsibility for providing documentation of their disability and for requested accommodations or services, and advocate on their own behalf (Sahlen and Lehmann 2006; Scott 1991). It is not unusual for there to be a gap between the assessment information collected under IDEA and the disability documentation required by colleges under the ADA or Section 504 (Sitlington and Payne 2004).

A third piece of federal law makes the situation even more complicated by explicitly creating barriers to parental involvement in college. The Family Educational Rights and Privacy Act (FERPA) gives parents certain rights to their children's education records through high school, but when students turn eighteen or begin postsecondary education, those rights transfer from the parents to the students themselves. College students' educational records are private. As a result, college faculty and staff are precluded from even talking about students with parents unless a student provides explicit written permission to the college to share specific information.

The rub here is that although parents helped their children choose colleges partly on the basis of the colleges' ability to provide appropriate disability services, youths were not always willing or prepared to pick up their rights and use them. David Engel and Frank Munger (2003) are hopeful that young adults who grow up benefiting from rights under IDEA may be more likely to engage with rights due to increased rights consciousness, but engagement with rights has proved to be complicated by developmental issues. Given a choice about using disability services, many youths planned not to use them if they could help it. This reluctance stemmed both from developmental issues faced by young adults more generally and from issues specific to being an individual labeled as having a disability. Adult disability rights often did not fit students' advocacy skills, their perceptions of their own needs, or the new identities that they wanted to forge for themselves in college, resulting in developmental mismatches.[4]

Developmental Mismatches

The ADA and Section 504 require that students identify themselves as having a disability to staff in the office that handles disability services and to provide documentation to substantiate their request for accommodations or services. This system puts the student in the driver's seat—students must actually pick up their rights, explain and document their needs, negotiate with disability services staff, and then notify each of their professors individually of their approved accommodations at the beginning of each semester. Students may find this process intimidating and time consuming, particularly because their parents typically did most or all of the advocacy work for them in high school. In fact, that was the norm. For example, Anna explained that she and her parents would talk about her needs before her IEP meetings and then her parents would explain to the special education staff the services she needed. Her parents were the front-line advocates, "because I had a hard time talking to the school about what I needed because I didn't really know unless my parents helped me figure it out."

Students who were on their own at college could find it difficult to use their rights under the ADA, particularly if they had no practice in advocating for themselves. Mica's experiences illustrate how daunting this can be. She had used her power wheelchair to get around her high school in Massachusetts, which had a somewhat spread-out campus, so she thought nothing of starting college on an open campus in New Hampshire. Everything was fine until it snowed.

MICA: I really wasn't prepared, because when I got there, because as I grew up I was so independent, like I did everything for myself, I never needed any outside services [except transportation], like I mentioned, so when I got there I was like, OK, this could work, just be my room, my kitchen's halfway across campus, you know. And as the weather started to pick up, because I was up in the mountains, so then that's when everything started to crumble. And when I got there I didn't like it because it was almost as if I wasn't there. Because like I wasn't going to class because I couldn't get to class, like my teachers were giving me a hard time so then I was like, who do I contact for this? Like they were failing me, I was like, oh no.

VALERIE: Is there a disability services office on campus?

MICA: There was and I did go there and they took my information, they said we're going to contact the woman. And she actually—because I lived in a new building because it was the most accessible and they said her office is actually right below your floor. And I said, "Why didn't somebody tell me that straight from the beginning?" I said, "Here I am going here, here, here," you know?

Mica finally connected with the disability services officer at the college, who did intervene with Mica's professors. However, that intervention did not solve all Mica's problems; it just eased her class attendance issue. When Mica pressed the officer further about how she could physically adapt to the environment and develop strategies to get around campus, she said the officer explained they were trying to do their best.

> [But] it would snow and they wouldn't plow for like three, four hours. I said, "Why is it taking so long?" I said, "It doesn't take this long where I come from." And she's like, "You're from Massachusetts, you're from the city, this is like boonish." She said, "It takes people time to come out and we only have a couple of people for the whole town." And I was just like, "For the whole town?" I was like, "That's not very good." And I said, "What are my chances of continuing?" And she said, "This is just the beginning of the winter," and I said, "Maybe then it's time for me to go home." And that's when I said, it's time for me to go home because I couldn't like do anything and I was stuck in my room all day. And like I would have friends go like get me meals and stuff because the cafeteria was way across campus.

Mica left that college. When we met, she was planning to start college again at an urban campus. She felt prepared this time. While in Boston, Mica had found mentors who helped her learn about her rights and how to use them. Staff at Easter Seals at the Massachusetts Rehabilitation Commission worked with her, and she felt that she had "more of a bigger advocacy under my belt." Although Mica's troubles engaging with disability services may be more difficult than usual, they give us insight into the challenges that students with disabilities may face at college. It will be difficult for students to advocate effectively for themselves if they are not aware of their rights and of their colleges' systems for accessing them, and do not have experience or mentoring on using their disability rights before arriving on campus. Developmentally, many youths may simply not have the skills needed to pick up their rights and use them, which may make their transition to college more difficult (Hadley 2006). Some professionals in the field have suggested that self-advocacy training be included in students' IEP transition plans in high school to give them the necessary skills and knowledge (Eckes and Ochoa 2005).

Students' desire for independence could also pose a developmental barrier, undercutting their use of disability rights. Kevin, a student with Asperger syndrome who wanted to study bioengineering, was initially reluctant to go to the disability services office when he began college. When asked about any accommodations he might need in college, he admitted: "I never want them, but I usually do need them." His mother, Karen, explained: "What we have found is Kevin has a very difficult time asking for help. And some of that is being a teenager. 'I can do it on my own.' He will either not tell me what's going on or tell me how he wished it was but it isn't." Kevin wanted to handle everything on his own but had gotten into a bind during his first semester. He had missed a lot of classes and ended up on academic probation. After this difficulty, he agreed to work to establish some accommodations, such as lenience with attendance and separate test time. Kevin had come to the conclusion that "it's better to have the option [to take tests separately]. More just the cavalry in my back pocket that I can use if I need it. When I don't need it, I have it, and when I have it, I don't need it." Knowing that he had the option to use the accommodations was helpful to him; they provided a safety net if he did experience difficulty in the future. His mother had been a strong advocate for him in special education, describing herself as very hard-headed during IEP meetings. She was initially unaware of his difficulties in college. When she found out, Karen told Kevin that advocating for himself was a form of independence. She explained: "He'll say, 'Okay, how do I do the conversation?' And we run it. Because I really—I don't want to run his life. I really don't want to run his life, but unfortunately I'm the one that's kind of straightening out the mess. So that he can get through. So this would be the accommodation. They said that he asked for it and they said 'We can't do that unless we get a note from a doctor.'" Kevin viewed going to disability services and requesting accommodations as asking for help, which made him dependent upon adults at the college. Karen was attempting to reframe Kevin's use of disability rights as an independent, adult endeavor, and was coaching him to use them on his own without her assistance.

In a related vein, many youths looked to college as an opportunity to test themselves and see what they were capable of doing without supports. When my research assistant, Lexie, asked Elaine, who had a physical condition, if she might need any accommodations in college, she responded: "I might. I don't know. There's a lot of pride issue with me in that because I tend to not do well with people being like, 'Oh, let me help you.' I'm like, 'No! I can do it!' And that was the biggest thing I had to learn . . . , to ask for help. It was just like that kind of thing. So I'm trying to keep in mind it's okay to not overdo it. And by nature, I would overdo things. I would definitely say, okay, I want to take six classes, because most people take five. And when I should be taking maybe four or something." Joseph also wanted to strike out on his own, to see if the adaptations that he had developed in high school were sufficient before turning to any supports or accommodations a college might provide. His mother, Ursula, explained that "he's very aware that he needs to be where there are services for him. And he said, 'I don't need structure,' he said, 'because that's what I had here [at high school] for three years.' And he said, 'That's why I came here, because I needed the services and I came here to get them. And I don't think I need them in college.'" She had convinced Joseph that he needed to go to a school with a good writing center. He agreed that it was a good idea but hoped that he would not need the help.

Negotiations between Hermione and her mother about Hermione's use of disability services had reached an impasse on the weekend before she started college. When Lexie asked Hermione if she planned on having any contact with disability services at school, she responded: "Well, I guess, I don't know. I'll just sort of see how it goes and if I think it will be a good idea, then I will. So I don't really know." Hermione had a Section 504 plan in high school that provided specific adaptations for Asperger syndrome. She explained that her mother wanted her to "transfer my 504 to college," but that her father felt that was unnecessary. Hermione's mother, Roberta, was incredibly frustrated with Hermione's refusal to identify herself as a student with a disability at college. Roberta had repeatedly tried to persuade her daughter to change her mind and had asked other adults to lobby her as well. Roberta described how she had talked with the husband of one of her friends, who was a professor. The husband "had actually written Hermione a letter saying, 'There's no shame in using accommodations, and I have students who I do this, this, and this for them.' And it just didn't do any good."

Disability services had become a point of contention in Hermione's transition to college, with Hermione holding fast and Roberta trying any tactic she could think of to make certain that Hermione had a safety net on campus. Roberta explained: "I have a friend who's a school psychologist, and she was saying I should call up her advisor, and without disclosing anything, just say, 'I have these concerns.' . . . But I can't say too much. It's like I can't mention the Asperger. But I can just say, 'She has some organizational difficulties, that kind of thing. Just keep an eye on her.'" Roberta's fear stemmed from knowing other students with Asperger syndrome who had begun college, only to drop out. She did not want that to happen to her daughter. Hermione's desire to test her capabilities without supports seemed to have won out, at least at that moment. Students desired independence and the opportunity to explore their true capabilities without supports, regardless of the type of disability they experienced, posing developmental barriers to the use of disability rights.

Stigma

Stigma was a barrier to the use of disability rights among the youths with hidden disabilities (learning disabilities and Asperger syndrome) alone. Most of the youths with physical or sensory disabilities had visible conditions, either through the physical appearance of their bodies or through the use of assistive devices such as canes or wheelchairs (see Goffman 1963). Occasionally, the evidence of a disability was more subtle, such as Darren's being hard of hearing, but his disability became apparent fairly quickly through social interaction. Youths with learning disabilities had the most potential to pass as not disabled after leaving high school. This option was not available to youths with physical or sensory disabilities, or to youths with intellectual disabilities.

Several youths with hidden disabilities and their parents spoke specifically about the stigma that could result from being labeled as having a disability. They had certainly felt this stigma while they were in high school, in association with the special education label. In elementary and secondary school, they had no choice about taking on a disability label—the adults in their lives had made that choice for them. While there were certainly benefits associated with these labels in the form of educational services and supports through IDEA, youths also experienced their costs, particularly social costs as their typically developing peers excluded them socially.

Girls were more likely to experience social isolation by their peers in high school. Anna, who had a learning disability, experienced the most extreme form of this isolation. She reported having no friends at all at her local public high school. Her mother followed her around school for a day and found that she spoke to just one other person, when a teacher asked a question in class and Anna answered it. This, and some complications regarding the supports that Anna was receiving, prompted Anna's parents to have her placed in a private school for students with disabilities, where she was accepted and was successful both academically and socially. At her new school, Anna said: "I got to know everybody and I made a lot of friends. I knew all the juniors and seniors and some of the other kids."

Boys were more likely to experience bullying from other boys. Joseph was a popular kid at his school until he received a diagnosis of a learning disability. Then his social position changed rapidly. One day in a science class, another student wrote "SPED" after his name on a list of lab partners. Carl, who also had a learning disability, was physically bullied by other students at high school to the point that he was afraid to go to school and "had some anxiety issues and stuff." Carl was eventually moved to a private school, where he "got a lot of respect. The whole environment there. Everyone there has been picked on at some point and, so they know what it's like and they know not to do it." Sandy, who had a physical condition, was bullied on the way to school. Kids threw ice balls at him, and the school eventually had a bus bring him back and forth to school. These are the more extreme examples of negative social consequences that youths experienced as a result of having disabilities. Ivan, a professional whose brother had a disability, acknowledged that bullying and social exclusion were the price of inclusion paid by youths with learning disabilities and Asperger syndrome who were in mainstream classrooms. Ivan explained that "if the attitudes weren't there, then that would not be a cost that individuals have to bear of being included. And in some instances, parents are just taking their kids out and putting them in special schools as a result." Often, the social exclusion was more subtle than outright bullying. It is not surprising therefore that youths might be reluctant to disclose having a disability upon entering to college if they perceived that they had a choice about it.[5]

Youths with hidden disabilities had the opportunity to jettison their disability labels upon entering college. They were not eager to pick up the labels voluntarily and put them back on. Audrey, who had a condition that resulted in a learning disability, just wanted to fit in with other students at high school and hid her condition from her peers. Her mother, Lisa, explained that "she doesn't like anybody to know that she has any kind of— I don't know. Hopefully, she would agree with [going to disability services]. I don't know. But I'm not paying for college unless she does. I'm not wasting my money to have her go and sit in a class that she can't comprehend and that she flunks because she can't get it without any help." Carl, who was also a junior with a learning disability, was reluctant to disclose and use disability services in college, but his mother, Kerry, convinced him to be open to using them. Kerry said that, initially, "he kind of didn't even want to go [to the disability services office during college visits] because he doesn't want anyone to know he has disabilities." Carl voiced his ambivalence about identifying himself as a student with a disability: "A few of my friends have gone on and tried to challenge themselves [by not using disability services], and a couple of my friends are being successful and they're not treated like they're different by professors and stuff because of that. And so that would be ideal. Having said that, I will have a computer. I will have books on tape through services, not through the school. I have a couple of services right now that I use to get free books on CD and books on tape. And I'll get textbooks and stuff so that I can do all my work, because I'm a really slow reader, which is another reason I don't read very much. So, yes, I will need that to get through all my work."

After intense discussions with his mother, Carl had grudgingly agreed to identify himself to the disability services office at college. However, to prevent his professors from knowing that he had a disability, he was not planning to activate his disability rights by requesting accommodations in his classes unless it became absolutely necessary. Carl saw the disability label as a stigma, while his mother saw it as triggering a safety net that Carl might need if he faced challenges in college that he had not anticipated: "Again, that's why sometimes they have to fall on their face. If that's what you want to do, I'm okay with that. But if you start to have trouble in October or November, then . . . they're at least knowing what's going on. If they start to see you suffering, then it's time that they're going to say to you, now it's time, you must do this. And then you'll know you can because you already have your file. But if you don't have a file, then you can't, and you'll get nothing." One key difference between Carl and his mother's perspectives is that it was Carl who had borne the brunt of bullying and therefore the cost of being identified as a student with a disability. Even though Kerry knew of the extent of the bullying, she was certain that it was worth the associated benefits to pursue disability rights in college. Carl felt that it was not worth the cost to him personally, in terms of his identity as a college student. Eventually, Carl and Kerry reached a compromise— Carl agreed to identify himself as a student with a disability at the disability services office, so that the option of using services would be open to him if it was needed. But as he indicated, he would not let his professors know about his disability unless he felt that he really needed the accommodations. What Carl did not know was that accommodations cannot be granted retroactively. If he did decide to activate his accommodations in a class midsemester, those accommodations would apply to his future assignments but not to work that he had already done for the class.

Adam, a professional who had a disability and worked with transition-age youths in a community-based organization, empathized with students' reluctance to disclose their disabilities in college: "Right, because now they're exposing themselves, whereas if people didn't know they had a disability, now they know. Then people start having these assumptions about you and things of that nature." Formal disability labeling is required under Section 504 and the ADA to ensure that students are entitled to disability rights and that appropriate adaptations and accommodations are provided. However, youths perceive that this labeling comes at the cost of both their self-image as independent adults and their worry about how others, particularly professors and peers, will perceive them.

Flying under the Disability Rights Radar

Either in addition to the use of formal disability services or as an alternative to them, some youths with hidden disabilities and their parents built informal strategies that sometimes allowed students to fly under the radar of disability systems on campus. Some of these strategies came with stiff financial costs, while others could actually save money while taking performance pressure off students. On the frugal side, several youths, including Kevin, planned to start at a community college and later transfer to a four-year college. Tuition costs loomed large in most parents' minds, and attending community college for the first two years reduced the cost of their child's college education. When I asked Nellie if her daughter, who had Asperger syndrome, was college bound, she replied: "Oh, yes. One way or another she's going to college, which I've been trying to explain to her that since college is so very expensive, it might be kind of nice to take some classes at a community college first, and then go to a four-year college. But first, get some classes. See what you like and don't like. And then go on with a background, because it's so expensive to go to college." With this strategy, students could explore and get their footing in college in the first year or two at a much lower financial cost. This approach allowed students to adjust to college more gradually and transfer to a four-year college after deciding on a specific course of study.

Another strategy was to take a reduced course load. Elyse, whose son Coleman wanted to go to college and eventually into the video game industry, was concerned about attending college full-time. They were "talking about maybe a reduced course load, trying to keep it—reduce the frustration or the demands a little bit the first semester, just so that he can figure out how it works. Because all of that can just be kind of confusing." Although Elyse saw this as a temporary strategy to ease her son's transition to college, some parents were considering a "five-year plan," in which students would take reduced course loads all the way through college. This strategy would ease students' transition to college and help them keep up their grade point averages but would result in higher financial costs to students and their families. Megan, a professional who worked with youths in high school, knew a student who "had been going to a school and taking two courses [a semester] for the last four years. A regular school. It's like a fortune." This strategy was not affordable for many families, but was more affordable if youths attended public colleges.

Although some students and parents planned on reduced course loads in advance, students might find themselves having to drop courses in the middle of the semester. In his first semester at a community college, Kevin had signed up for a full course load, but he had to withdraw from one class and take an incomplete in another when he faced some class attendance issues and fell behind on his work. The approach helped Kevin complete his other classes but resulted in a *W* (for Withdrawn late in the semester) on his transcript. One *W* is certainly not a problem, but if students repeatedly drop classes, their transcripts begin to look like Swiss cheese. Students who employ this strategy repeatedly may incur financial and other costs. They may pay for part of the classes that they did not complete (with the percentage of the tuition paid increasing as the semester continues), and it becomes apparent to anyone who reads their transcripts that something is affecting their academic performance. This approach thus may not allow students to fly under the disability radar completely and may result in damage to students' permanent academic records. Transcripts can be important for applying for graduate school and jobs, so there may be long-term consequences. Each of these informal strategies allows youths to keep their disabilities hidden to varying degrees in college, but they may come with financial and academic costs.

Goodness of Fit

Disability rights did not seem to fit the prospective college students particularly well. Some of the mismatch is the result of developmental issues, including the need for advocacy skills and young adults' perception of rights as a form of continued dependence upon adults, and some is the result of students wanting to escape any stigma associated with disability that they may have experienced in high school. It is important to note, however, that college students with disabilities are certainly not the only group of people that is reluctant to use disability rights. Parents of children who receive disability services for their infants and toddlers under IDEA and adults who are eligible for protection under the ADA are also often reluctant to engage with disability rights as remedies when they encounter difficulties (see Engel and Munger 2003; Leiter 2004b; Price, Gerber, and Mulligan 2007). Rights may be available, but their effectiveness depends upon individuals picking them up and using them.

This brings us back to the role that colleges may play in this rights-based approach to improving access to college. Section 504 and the ADA have transformed the way colleges and universities interact with students with disabilities. Students now have rights, and institutions have certain responsibilities to provide accessibility and accommodations. But subtly, some colleges create climates that are less welcoming to students with disabilities. By not including disability services at open houses and other recruiting forums, colleges create a barrier to information about disability services on campus and send a message that having a disability is not a typical experience on their campus. Colleges' disability services websites, a typical source of information for prospective students and their parents, can be lively and informative, bureaucratic and vague, or anything in between. These subtler signals can be important. Students may face barriers to the use of their rights when they do attempt to use them, including colleges' lack of understanding, communication, and coordination, as well as physical accessibility problems (Dowrick et al. 2005; West et al. 1993). These barriers would be difficult for any student to address alone, just after leaving home. Youth's reluctance to identify themselves to disability services may be reduced by making the college climate more welcoming, acknowledging that there are many students with disabilities on campus, raising faculty awareness of disability issues, and emphasizing performance goals rather than needs when reaching out to students (see Dehart 2008; Hartman-Hall and Haaga 2002).

Getting into college is one thing. Completing college is another. Although students with disabilities are entering college in greater numbers, they are less likely than their peers without disabilities to complete college. Students with disabilities were less likely to persist in their post-secondary programs—53 percent, compared with 64 percent of students without disabilities (NCES/OERI 2000). More welcoming implementation of disability rights by colleges and more effective use of rights among students might improve these students' chances of success.

6

The End of Entitlement

Two of the most important cultural markers of adulthood in the United States are turning eighteen and graduating from high school. For some youths with disabilities, leaving high school happens later as a result of federal special education legislation. The Individuals with Disabilities Education Act (IDEA) allows some students to stay in special education until age twenty-two, subject to state law. Those whose disabilities are severe enough to make them eligible for adult services and make it difficult for them to obtain competitive employment may remain in high school until they "age out" of their entitlement to special education. (The exact age varies from state to state.) Few students with disabilities stay in high school until they age out—most graduate, drop out, or leave with certificates. Those with intellectual disabilities are more likely than others to stay until they age out of special education, and those with multiple disabilities are the most likely to leave school by this route.[1]

In effect, special education law draws an additional outer boundary around adolescence for youths who stay in special education until they age out of their entitlement. This boundary is the last one that some youths with intellectual disabilities must pass before being considered adults completely. Youths who stay in school until the maximum age allowed under this law exist in a kind of legal and social limbo: they are have reached the legal age of majority yet are still technically high school students and the responsibility of their local school districts.

Delayed Departures

All states provide special education to children through age seventeen. The upper age limit varies by state after age seventeen, ranging from eighteen to twenty-six years.[2] Michigan provides special education for the longest time by far, covering youths until their twenty-sixth birthdays. The lowest age varies, with fuzzy boundaries in some states. For example, students are entitled to special education through age eighteen in Montana, although school districts may serve them through the school year in which they turn twenty-one. In Maine, the boundary is set at nineteen, with youths allowed to start the school year only if they have not yet reached age twenty.[3]

Under Massachusetts state law (Chapter 766), students with disabilities are entitled to remain in high school until they graduate or until their twenty-second birthday, even if it falls in the middle of the school year. Of the twenty-one students with intellectual disabilities and the five with intellectual plus physical disabilities who were included in this study, all but one planned to stay in special education until their twenty-second birthday. Their parents were aware that their children's entitlement to special education ended at age twenty-two. The youths were staying until their entitlement ended to gain academic, vocational, and independent living skills during the additional years of schooling and because eligibility for adult systems did not usually start until age twenty-two—adult services were timed to start when the entitlement under special education law ended. Turning twenty-two is therefore a major marker of adulthood among many youths with intellectual and multiple disabilities in Massachusetts.

Those who age out of high school leave individually, unlike those who graduate from high school in a cohort with their peers. On the last day of their twenty-first year, they are the responsibility of their local school districts. The very next day, they are officially adults, according to special education law, and no longer entitled to a public education. All is determined by the timing of their birthday. In the United States, one's eighteenth birthday brings the right to vote and one's twenty-first birthday bring the right to purchase alcohol, two legal and cultural markers of contemporary adulthood. But for some youths with intellectual disabilities, their twenty-second birthday is a key marker of adulthood too, when they leave special education and enter the adult world fully. Adulthood as a social and policy category is regulated partly by special education law among youths with intellectual and multiple disabilities.

Upon exiting special education, young adults may be eligible for adult services through state agencies if their local school districts determine that their disabilities are severe enough. To be eligible for adult disability services in Massachusetts, students must be receiving special education paid for by the Commonwealth of Massachusetts, need continuing services when they graduate from special education or turn twenty-two, and "be unable to work competitively (without specialized supports) for more than twenty hours per week at the time of leaving school" (MDMR 2008). If the school district deems a youth eligible for adult services, then according to state law the youth should be referred to the relevant adult agency two years before the student's exit from special education.[4] Depending on the nature of their disabilities, youths may be referred to the Massachusetts Commission for the Blind, the Massachusetts Commission for the Deaf and Hard of Hearing, or the Massachusetts Rehabilitation Commission. Those with intellectual disabilities who have documented IQs of seventy or lower may be eligible for adult services from the Department of Developmental Services (DDS). All the youths with intellectual disabilities in this study had been determined by their local school districts to be eligible for DDS services. These state adult disability agencies may provide transition counseling in the years before a youth's exit from special education but typically do not assume responsibility for providing services until the school district's legal responsibility under special education law has been fulfilled.

How did these young people feel about their delayed departures from high school? Most took it in stride. It was what they had prepared for and what their peers with disabilities at school were also experiencing, so for them it was simply their route out of high school. A handful were aware that they had missed a milestone on the route to adulthood when their age peers graduated from high school and they remained. In each of these instances, they came to this conclusion by comparing themselves to typically developing youths and realizing that they were leaving high school later. Siblings and age peers were benchmarks whom they relied on to give them a sense of where they stood relative to traditional milestones in adolescence and young adulthood. Three youths explicitly compared themselves to their siblings—it was particularly irksome if a younger sibling passed them by developmentally, leaving high school before they did and going on to college. Sergeant had two brothers, one older and one younger. He expected his older brother to leave high school ahead of him but did not expect his younger brother also to do so. Sergeant wanted to be more independent in part because his younger brother was in college. Isabella also yearned for more independence. When she was asked where she thought she'd live after she finished high school, she replied: "College." Lexie, my research assistant, followed up.

LEXIE: At college?

ISABELLA: Yeah, my sister.

LEXIE: Your sister lives at college?

ISABELLA: Yeah.

LEXIE: Do you want to live at college like her?

ISABELLA: Yeah!

Isabella's sister had started college a few months earlier, "far, far away." Isabella wanted to have the same kind of life her sister was having. Her mother explained: "Her sister just started college and she's all—Isabella says she wants to go to college and live in a dorm."

Sarah had similar short-term goals—she wanted to go to college, live in a dorm, and have a computer and a cell phone (especially the cell phone), just like her brother. She was commuting to a nearby transition program for youths with disabilities, having been placed there by the local school district because her high school felt it could no longer address her needs adequately. When Sarah asked her parents when she would go to college too, her father, Peter, said that "we tell her that [her transition program] is college," because "that's what she wants more than anything, is to go away like her brother." Another young woman, Mary, felt that she had been left behind because she had been the team manager for her high school's volleyball team for several years. She helped the team work on skills during practices and attended the games. Mary mentioned that "all of the seniors on my volleyball team are going off to college" and had asked her mother about why she had to stay in high school after they left. It still didn't make sense to her that they had moved on but she had not.

In contrast, none of the few youths who attended residential transition programs mentioned feeling left behind, and their parents did not report this feeling either. These young people were living away from home, independent of their families, and therefore may have felt that they were having a "real" college experience, unlike those who commuted to transition programs from home or were still attending their local high schools. In social terms, youths felt left behind when they were still living at home and were aware that siblings or age peers had left to attend college or live on their own. Eager to move on to adult life, they did not always understand why they were still at home and attending "high school."

Transition Time

What happens in those additional transition years? The answer varies greatly, based upon a youth's abilities, future plans, and service needs and the school district's approach to providing opportunities during this transition phase of high school. About half the youths with intellectual disabilities spent their transition years at their local high schools, and the other half spent them at private schools, public vocational schools, or public collaborative programs (regional programs that serve youths with developmental disabilities from multiple towns located near each other). Hannah described her transition program as "a kind of place to get ready for the outside world."

Those who had intellectual disabilities engaged in three types of activities during this transition period: vocational exposure and training, life skills training, and academic classes. Vocational training was stressed, as schools helped students prepare for employment after high school. Earlier in the transition phase, students would often experiment with different jobs. Sometimes they were sent out to various work sites for a day or two, to try out the work and the setting. The jobs lasted a few weeks or months. Donnie was trying out two jobs through his school's vocational exploration program. He sorted mail at a local hospital and gathered carts and bagged groceries at a local supermarket.

By the time they had turned twenty, most students knew what kind of work they wanted to do and were gaining solid experience. Mary wanted to work with young children when she completed high school. She had worked part-time for four years in a kindergarten classroom at her local school. Currently, she was there on Mondays and Tuesdays. On Wednesdays through Fridays, she focused on independent living skills, such as shopping and cooking, and English and math literacy classes. Jessica wanted to be a professional cook and was attending a vocational school that provided culinary training. She had chosen cooking as a career after her previous school took her on "a tour of like fifteen things, and cooking was the one I saw I liked the best." She liked working with food but was also attracted because the work "was more moving around than sitting," which fit her high energy level. At her school, she worked three days a week and took vocational classes two days a week. (This vocational focus was the result of Jessica's parents' advocacy work. Before attending this vocational school, Jessica had spent her days with other students with disabilities in what was essentially a storage room in her local high school, surrounded by four stoves and boxes of textbooks.)

In some schools, preparation for employment involved ramping up from doing jobs at the school such as mail, recycling, and so on, to going out into jobs in the community. Community jobs were sometimes volunteer positions, such as helping with Meals on Wheels deliveries, but occasionally included paid placements, such as working at Starbucks, Target, Marshalls, or other office and retail settings. Many schools maintained relationships with employers that allowed them to develop work slots that were given to students while they were in school. Once a student finished school, the slot would be given to another student. Beth's slot at Starbucks was coveted because of the environment and the food, and several other students were eager for her to transition so that the slot would open up. Occasionally, schools helped students get part-time paid employment with competitive employers in the community. Donnie worked at Marshalls, stocking. Sean's teacher helped him get a part-time job at Target. He enjoyed working there and hoped to pick up more hours once he was done with school.

Life skills classes focused on independent living skills, such as cooking, banking, and shopping. Sean lived in a town whose high school had a comprehensive life skills curriculum that included transportation training—he was taught how to use the Ride (a paratransit system for people with disabilities), buses, and the T (the subway system in the Boston metropolitan area). William attended a "community independence" class, in which his "best teachers" took students out into the local community to do shopping and other errands such as visiting the local library. In her community skills class, Laura's "favorite place to go would have to be Stop 'n' Shop. [*Laughs.*] To get groceries and all that kind of stuff. Make a list and buy some stuff for my mom. It's really kind of cool and I really like that."

The academic courses that youths took were largely practical in nature, helping them improve their reading and their math skills. However, three youths with intellectual disabilities, Alan, Kayla, and Sarah, were included in regular academic classes during their transition period in high school after age eighteen. This sounds terrific at first, but in practice, their schools seemed to be warehousing them, fulfilling the letter of special education law but creating no educational opportunities that matched the students' interests or abilities. Sarah attended regular high school classes with an aide for several years after turning eighteen, including science, acting out when she got bored because she could not follow the material. Her behavior began to pose challenges in the classroom, and Sarah's aide at first responded by removing her from the classroom and taking Sarah for long walks when she got bored in class. Eventually, Sarah's school district decided to place her in a private transition program because they did not have appropriate programming. Although Sarah would prefer to be in college like her brother, she did like her transition program much more than her high school, and her parents felt that it was giving her skills she would need later in life. At first glance, Sarah's participation in regular high school classes might look like integrated mainstreaming, but the substance of the classes was not accessible to her and did not meet her interests or needs for after high school.

Kayla's high school had placed her in Chinese and Spanish classes because she had taken and passed all the other academic classes offered and could not take them again. Kayla's aunt described how the school had "modified" these language classes so that Kayla could participate: "Why don't I tell you when the teacher modified the curriculum for Kayla. Spanish is the one thing I had tangible proof. I knew they weren't just modifying it, they were passing it. She would give twenty vocabulary words that everyone had to copy off the bulletin board. [Kayla] would get down maybe ten of them. Of those ten, she had maybe three spelled right.

So if she could do those three words, she passed. I'm sorry, that's not modification." Kayla and her aunt pressured the school to change Kayla's classes. As a result, Kayla was taking science, math, and reading classes that focused more on functional literacy, plus life skills and vocational classes that fostered Kayla's interest in doing culinary work. Kayla was now engaged in preparing for her career goal of becoming a dietary aide.

Alan's situation was more complicated. Alan had taken wood shop for five years even though it was just a hobby and he did not plan on pursuing woodworking as a career, and he had been training to do culinary work even though he did not like the work and did not want to pursue it after school. Suddenly, Alan's high school placed him in regular science and gym classes during this school year because he needed them to fulfill his school's graduation requirements. Alan had just passed the Massachusetts Comprehensive Assessment System (MCAS), the state's standardized achievement exam, which meant that he was slated to graduate at the end of the year. Most youths with intellectual disabilities were not in a position to pass MCAS and graduate. The MCAS exam is a gate of sorts for all youths seeking a high school diploma. For transition-age youths who are receiving special education services, it is also a gate out of special education. Youths are entitled to a public education until they turn twenty-two or graduate, whichever happens first. Those who graduated were required to leave high school and could not stay until they aged out at age twenty-two.

Alan's passing MCAS meant that he would graduate with a high school diploma, thereby ending his entitlement to special education services. Alan was excited about graduating. He felt that he had been in school long enough and wanted to move on to a job. When I asked his mother, Tonya, about the exam, she replied: "He passed both of them [math and language arts]. The teacher said, 'He did a good job guessing, but he passed.' I said, 'You know what? He's going to graduate with a diploma.'" Tonya was proud of this accomplishment but was unsure exactly how it had occurred. During the interview, she pulled out a copy of the most recent assessment the school had done to determine Alan's eligibility for DDS services. The assessment stated clearly that Alan's academic skills were between the second and third grade, which was completely inconsistent with his either passing MCAS or completing four years of high school English and math. Tonya explained that during the IEP meeting after Alan passed the exam, the special education director from the school district told her and Alan not to worry because DDS would provide employment support services after Alan graduated. An advocate from the local Arc who attended the IEP meeting apparently questioned this. Tonya reported that the advocate said that "it's not always happening until they're twenty-two." The special education director replied that it would be okay because they were telling DDS a year in advance. Tonya was reassured: "It's really all new to me. But all I know is I've got one mom that's going to make sure that it's either going to be through this organization or another one. If they don't follow through, it will have to be. And so far they seem to be so supportive, I can't see there being any problem." Although Tonya felt that someone would help Alan after he graduated, she did not understand completely that Alan *might* be eligible for services but that there was no guarantee he would receive them before the typical age of twenty-two. Alan could fall between the cracks between high school and DDS adult services by leaving high school earlier. There is no entitlement to adult DDS services for anyone, and DDS did not typically provide services to individuals before they turned twenty-two.

Is Alan's experience a rare occurrence, or are other youths with intellectual disabilities who initially plan to leave at age twenty-two also experiencing "early bird specials," in which they pass MCAS and graduate even though their intellectual disabilities would seem to make that impossible? I asked the professionals whom I interviewed if they had ever heard of students leaving under these circumstances. Bernie, who had worked for a state agency, said that yes, he did come across them occasionally: "Tragically, without getting into which communities these are, they're also the communities where I see a higher percentage of kids leaving school before the age of twenty-two. And to me, that is just the worst combination that you could possibly ask, to have kids leaving before they need to. But they're leaving because they're really not getting what they need. So they're coming out, they're young, they're much less mature, and they're really unprepared for jobs and that whole—all the attendant skills." Bernie told me that he just couldn't understand how some of the youths he had met had passed MCAS. When I asked Norma, another professional, about early bird specials, she said that she had seen multiple cases, adding: "How can you pass MCAS? Even with an IQ of seventy, how can someone pass MCAS?" When I asked her how it was happening, she said: "I don't know. I don't know how."

From Entitled to Eligible

In Massachusetts, on the last day of their twenty-first year, youths are entitled to a public education through special education law. On the first day of their twenty-second year, they may be eligible for adult services. This shift from entitled to eligible is enormous. Youths were largely unaware of the magnitude of the shift that awaited them. They looked forward to finally finishing high school. It was parents who worried about the timing and substance of the change from entitled to eligible. As Rochelle explained: "With special education, you know. It's a law. With [DDS], it's not an entitlement, basically. We'll give your son as much as we can, but we can't grow to meet his needs."

Parents did not always find the special education system easy but it was a known quantity—after years of experience, parents knew what to expect and what their rights were within that system. Certainly by the end of high school there were relatively few surprises. Then transition loomed. As Marie described it: "Up until a certain point, it's all really mapped out, and you can go to trainings, you can find out exactly 'these are your rights' and all that, and all of a sudden, surprise, back out into a brand-new world. Who knows what's going to happen?" Reflecting back on special education, Melinda felt that she and her daughter Mary were pampered in comparison to the adult system they were about to face: "Everything was laid out for us. They tell us. We were taken care of, services provided. The options are fairly limited. It doesn't take much to talk with a few other parents and find out, you know, you can get this kind of services through the school. But then it seems like all of a sudden you break out of the school and there's this world out there. I don't have any sense at all—I may be wrong, but I don't have a sense that the options and the resources are packaged in such a way that I can access them. So that's really scary to me." Parents whose children were approaching their twenty-second birthday described the transition to adult services as a "cliff," a "chasm," "falling off the table," and "springboarding off into the vast unknown of adult services," with youths being "thrown to the wind." Parents saw it as a free fall, and dreaded and feared the shift.

Parents coped with this fear in diverse ways. Some kept their heads down and hoped for the best. Some tried to adjust by continuing their

advocacy efforts, hoping that it would make a difference in the adult services provided by DDS. Cassandra took a "you can catch more bees with
honey than vinegar" approach to advocacy. She brought cookies to the
local DDS office, just as mothers several generations ago fed state legislators at luncheons. Cassandra said she had "made myself very known at the
local [DDS] office, not being cranky, not complaining. I have nothing to
complain about. Nothing's happened yet. But, you know, 'Have you seen
this recent picture of Missy?' And I'll take it in, drop it off. 'This is what
she's doing now.'" In contrast, Rachel and Jim took an aggressive
approach, hiring a lawyer and sending a letter to DDS in which they threat-
ened to sue because they were unhappy with the placement options
available to their son Sergeant. Just as in the parents' rights movement
described in chapter 2, parents' advocacy efforts ranged from homemade
food to legal challenges.

Parents worried about the quality of the services their children would
receive. When they asked other parents or staff at their children's schools
about adult services, they were always told not to expect the level or quality of services their children were currently receiving through special education. Statements like these only heightened parents' fears. Rochelle said
that when she asked the teachers at her son's school about adult services,
"I was told it's different. It scares you. 'You won't get what you've been
getting.' What does it mean?" When I asked Deb if she knew any parents
whose children had transitioned already, she replied: "Yeah, I do know
parents, and a lot of parents will say, 'Deb, they'll want to scoop him up,
they'll want to put him in an adult group home that has forty-, fifty-, sixty-
year [olds]. . . . They'll take them to Price Chopper and maybe he'll be able
to bag groceries some day, and it's going to be dismal.'" Tee-Tee, whose
son Eddie had both intellectual and physical disabilities, felt particularly
vulnerable because her son needed to be placed in a day program and she
was concerned about the care he would receive. Staff from Eddie's school
took her around to several programs, but she was far from impressed by
what she saw.

> So a lot of the program in which I was seeing was day care, pretty
> much. They sit there and twiddle their thumbs and they wait for
> time to, you know, go around. And they may have somebody come

in with music. Or they go to lunch. That gives them a different area to eat at. That pretty much was the basics! It was such big difference [from his school] and disappointment. . . . I was there and then I was watching myself because my son, he was in the group then, about eight adults, and then everybody was dependent. Everybody has diapers, so how can you manage it? . . . Basically they spend the seven or eight hours just changing diapers and feeding and that's that. That's not much. You know? That's not their fault, you know. It's somebody's fault.

From Tee-Tee's perspective, she had to trust a program with Eddie, whom she called "the most precious thing in my life." Eventually she did locate a program that she thought did a good job caring for participants, where there were regular recreational activities and some therapeutic care built into his day, and she was happy to think that Eddie was in good hands.

Gladys, whose son Sam also had intellectual and physical conditions, decided not to place him into a day program, electing to keep him at home full-time. Sam had transitioned out of special education just before I met them. He had complex medical needs and Gladys had visited day programs, as Tee-Tee had. Dissatisfied with the programs available, she opted out. Talking over coffee in her kitchen, Gladys said that she was committed to caring for Sam herself, with a little daily help from personal care attendants. But she was clearly exhausted as she sipped coffee while cooking and processing food that could be put into Sam's feeding tube. Keeping a young adult with significant medical needs at home is an option for families but may come with physical and emotional costs, especially to the primary caregiver.

Parents' worries about day programs were often grounded in past bad experiences with care—once burnt, it could be difficult for parents to trust new programs, worrying that their children would be neglected or harmed again. For example, Tee-Tee told a story about a school Eddie had attended when he was younger where they weren't changing his diaper. She sent him to school wearing a diaper that she had signed and he came home at the end of the day still wearing it. When youths were nonverbal, parents had to develop trust in a program, because they could not count on their children to tell them what did or did not happen each day. There was a heightened sense of vulnerability.

Parents whose children needed few supports were worried that their children's capabilities might mean that they would receive few or no services because other youths' needs exceeded theirs. Melinda worried that there might not be any transportation or employment supports for her daughter Mary. Without transportation support, Melinda would not be able to get Mary back and forth to work if she did obtain a job, because Melinda was working full-time. Mary also needed some job coaching to help her settle into a job and monitor her work. Without these services, Mary would not be able to keep a job and would have to stay at home all day, but she could not stay by herself safely. If Mary were home all day, Melinda would have to stop working and stay home too. This would have important social and financial consequences for the entire family. Patrick and Joan were hoping that there would be a program for their son Brent once he turned twenty-two; if not, Patrick assumed that he and Brent would be at home together. Patrick looked forward to Brent's company during the day, yet he really wanted Brent to have a more independent life.

The specter of youths being at home with nothing to do was especially troubling to youths and parents who had worked the hardest to develop abilities throughout childhood and adolescence. Hannah, who was a spokesperson for Special Olympics and hoped to continue working with the organization after turning twenty-two, had benefited from intensive services and educational programs throughout her life. She had received Early Intervention therapeutic services as an infant and toddler, experienced inclusion in elementary and middle school, and now attended a private transition program for youths with developmental disabilities. She was an articulate and active member of her school community. Her parents worried about what would follow when she turned twenty-two. Hannah said: "My dad wants me to just get out there and do something. Sitting here doing nothing, I waste my time." Her father, Dirk, said: "I think the saddest thing, to me, would be . . . you do all this work in grammar school, in middle school, in high school and now this, to end up at home watching TV and us carting her around. I mean, that's going to be a real loss to everybody that ever worked with her. So, yeah, it would be great if we could keep that going and build on it. The hard part is funding." He and his wife, Jean, were concerned that the years that Hannah was spending at her transition program could be the best years of her life. At school, Hannah had classes, many friends, and a boyfriend she liked very much. She was also gaining practical skills that would help her live more independently and be employed later. At home in her pleasant suburban community, she was dependent upon her parents to drive her places and felt isolated, with little social contact. Home for winter break, Hannah spent much of her time watching movies.

Hannah belongs to a generation of youths with intellectual disabilities who have achieved more than previous generations and often have skills and accomplishments that can translate into work and other contributions to their communities, both paid and unpaid. As a result of their efforts and resulting achievements, youths and their parents expect more from life than have earlier generations. Yet it was not clear if life would continue to bring opportunities for growth and achievement after their transition to adult service systems. Youths had envisioned much larger lives than staying home and watching TV all day, but transportation and other supports might not be available to facilitate employment and other meaningful adult activities outside the home. This situation—in which youths maximized their abilities throughout childhood and adolescence but could face limited adult opportunities after leaving high school—is like being all dressed up with no place to go.

Several affluent families ensured that their children would continue to have enriching experiences, would have someplace to go, even if they had to create the arrangements themselves. Rachel and Jim arranged for their son Sergeant and another young man with an intellectual disability to work part-time where they worshiped. Another mother, Angela, was working with a nonprofit organization called Toward Independent Living and Learning (TILL) to arrange for independent living supports for her son William, which she estimated would cost $40,000 per year, akin to sending William to college every year for the rest of his life. Middle-class and working-class families rarely had access to the social and financial resources needed to create such arrangements. They were therefore dependent upon the state agency DDS to provide opportunities when youths turned twenty-two—employment supports, transportation, and in some instances day programs (depending upon the nature of the youths' aspirations, abilities, and needs).

Turning Twenty-two

All twenty-six youths with intellectual disabilities included in this study were eligible for DDS services upon turning twenty-two and had been referred to DDS by their school districts. In each instance, someone had told the parents about their children's entitlement to special education until their twenty-second birthday—some parents knew as the result of workshops by local Arcs, the Federation for Children with Special Needs, or other organizations, while some learned from other parents or from employees of state agencies that provided adult services. Youths had a range of abilities and service needs. Some youths were able to work part-time in competitive employment without much or any support, some could work part-time but needed supports such as transportation and job coaching, and those with both intellectual and physical disabilities would attend day programs if they opted to receive services.

Advance planning was difficult, as adult services opportunities often depended on program slots being open at the moment an individual turned twenty-two. DDS contracts out services to a multitude of vendors, in addition to providing some support funding directly to families. School districts are mandated to initiate referrals to the adult service systems at least two years prior to transition, and all the parents reported that their children had been referred to DDS for services within that time frame. In the interim two years, DDS assigned a transition counselor to help youths plan for the future. These counselors met with families periodically to explain the adult system and discuss the youths' goals, resources, and needs. Some but not all transition counselors attended students' annual IEP meetings at their schools. Parents and transition professionals reported that the DDS transition counselors had very large caseloads, making it difficult for them to devote much attention to the youths in their caseloads until just before their transition to adult services.

Five of the twenty-six youths with intellectual disabilities had transitioned within a few months of participating in this study. In each of these cases, the actual moment of transition was very stressful for the youths and the parents, in part because of the unpredictability of placements available right up to the last moment. Rachel, who hoped that DDS would place her son in a group home told me: "In February, he graduated. We were told in maybe January to look at homes. I was pushing to do something before that, because we don't do things on the spur of the moment. We really have to research and look." Rachel and Jim wanted to look at places earlier but were unable to do so because DDS did not know which residences would actually be available when Sergeant turned twenty-two. Looking for adult service slots is similar to looking for apartments, in that it is typically not possible to look for a place to live a year before moving. Potential vacancies become known one to three months before they will be available. Sometimes vacancies open up even more quickly, at the last minute. In Beth's case, she transitioned to a day program practically overnight, her mother, Jane, explained.

JANE: I mean, we found out she had the program on Friday and she transitioned Monday, over the weekend.

VALERIE: Literally?

JANE: Over the weekend, because [DDS] wouldn't commit to, this is the final placement. And the school had to finish on her birthday which was on that Monday. . . . They sort of just waited till the very last minute to make that decision.

When parents asked transition counselors why it was not possible to plan earlier, the counselors said that program availability changes constantly. Bernie, a professional, explained:

You know, I struggle with families who want to see a house when their son or daughter is nineteen or twenty years old. And philosophically, we don't do that. I tell people, "These are people's homes, you know?" These aren't just buildings, this is where people live. And it's just not a polite thing to be traipsing through somebody's home and doing a tour. . . . You know, I don't show people programs they can't get in—that's day programs and residences. I will provide them with a list, they can look at anything they want. But my philosophy is I don't want to show something that is not going to be an option. What's the point? It's just an experience in frustration for a family. "Isn't this a beautiful home? Johnny can't go there. You know, he can't get in, it's full." So I don't do that kind of stuff, but part of the conversation around homes is that these are people's homes. We respect their home and we only go in and see the place if we're going to be offering you a place there. And the other part is, because families are like, "But yeah, what do they look like?" And my answer to that is, "They look like houses. It's not the building you're going to want to be interested in seeing, it's the agency and the people that are there. That's the part that's important." But it's a struggle. That uncertainty, it's unnerving to families.

If a youth and parents loved a program and the youth did not get in because no vacancies opened up, it could be bitterly disappointing. Barbara said of her and her daughter Carol's experience: "They're like, well, you can look now and see but everything could be changed, staffing or budget, program, it can be gone."

In fact, funding was *the* key issue in the provision of adult services upon transition. Youths in special education were entitled to a publicly funded education. Adults with intellectual disabilities who were eligible for adult services through DDS might receive all the services they and their families wanted, some of those services, or none of them. Tonya explained the "the big thing is the budget. I know with everything I've read, I've looked online for certain things, and everything is to be if there's money. And there seems to be a limited amount of money for these programs." Another mother, Marka, said: "That's the hard part, is, you know, you're trying to develop such a healthy vision for your child, but the response from agencies is no. And I understand why, they don't have the money. There's no funding." The adult disability service agencies, including DDS, are dependent on the annual state budget. The annual DDS budget is subject to constant change, depending on economic circumstances.

Parents understood this financial reality at an intellectual level—just like their own budgets, state money is finite. Once spent, it is gone. While upset about this financial situation, Jane knew why it occurred and how it translated into lost opportunities: "The adult system is just relying every year on the budget. You know? You're looking at the state budget where the school system is, like, okay, you know you have that entitlement. But the adult system, if they cut, the governor cuts out a couple line items, then it drastically affects your individual—you know, your child's future with their jobs, their placement, the number of days they can have a placement." Ziggy told me that while her daughter Yvonne's DDS transition counselor was pleasant, it was hard to hear the message that he delivered about funding. Yvonne, while eligible for services in a year, might not receive any for a while.

ZIGGY: We've been given an amazing runaround by DDS. Guardianship was an ordeal, SSI [Supplemental Security Income] is an ordeal, but you expect that. It starts, it ends. SSI keeps going on. There was a reason for that, because we wanted the health insurance for her. DDS has just been unbelievably frustrating.

VALERIE: Do you have a sense of what's going on?

ZIGGY: Money. Money. We live in a society that does not put an emphasis on folks like my daughter.

Just before I interviewed Ziggy, I heard that DDS had sent a letter to the families of youths who would be turning twenty-two in 2009 saying that there might be a gap in services for youths transitioning from special education to DDS that year. Ziggy had just received the letter and showed it to me, voicing her frustration that all her advocacy and her daughter's hard work might be for naught: "And what's the point? What's the point? Because you get to a point like that, and we have no clue if there is going to be money for her or not. . . . This is not a kid I can leave alone. What does that mean in terms of our life, and can we plan anything? Here, on the one hand, all these—you know, the Federation and all these people—'Oh, start planning early.' *For what?* For what reason?"

Faced with large numbers of youths transitioning to DDS and budget constraints, DDS was attempting to stretch the money as far as possible. Since 1999, DDS had received additional funding that allowed it to provide some services to all "turning twenty-two students" as a result of a lawsuit aimed at eliminating the waiting list for DDS services that had existed previously, according to the department's 2002 annual report. In 2002, according to that report, all 547 transitioning youths in Massachusetts received "at least day, family support, or transportation services, and about 25 percent of that class were offered residential services as well" (MDMR 2002, 5). By the time the youths in this study were transitioning to adult services, that funding had dried up.[5] Funding for public services in general had dried up, too, as youths transitioned in the midst of a severe recession. Maureen, a professional, explained: "At this point, here we are in the State of Massachusetts. And the entire economy everywhere around us is tanking. I'm waiting to hear about various cuts in services. And I don't know what's going to end up happening. I mean, I think, in an ideal world, there would've been a lot more money dumped into turning twenty-two by all the agencies. I don't think that happened this year, and I think what did happen is going to get cut." DDS's funding is vulnerable. The agency is subject to budget cuts, the same as other public services. Confronted by constrained resources, DDS is attempting to ration services without seeming to do so. With diminished resources, there is increased competition for services among adults with disabilities. Jane, a mother, explained that "the transition coordinator who's making all these recommendations, who's looking at the budget, obviously, and saying, if we spend all this on these kids, the next family coming down the road will have less." There is a zero-sum game at work in the adult disability service systems, which is being felt keenly by adults with intellectual disabilities and their families. There are finite agency budgets and those budgets are being cut repeatedly due to the recession. Under this system of service rationing, if one person gets more, someone else will get less. And some people will get no services at all.

Part of parents' concern around the timing of youths' exit from special education was grounded in wanting the best for their children. Parents wanted them to have the most opportunities for growth possible and looked to their children's schools to provide those opportunities. Not all parents of youths with intellectual disabilities know about their children's right to remain in publicly funded education until their entitlement ends and to receive assistance with learning independent living skills. The parents here knew about those rights. Some wanted their children to graduate from high school if they could, yet were told by other parents, teachers, and staff in state agencies that they should not allow them to do so because it would end the entitlement to special education before the youths' twenty-second birthday. Emma explained the tension she faced when trying to decide whether her daughter Ophelia should graduate or not: "People kept telling me 'Don't get a diploma, because they'll keep paying for whatever services she needs up until age twenty-two because of the deadline.'" On one hand, Emma wanted her daughter to graduate from high school, to have that achievement. On the other hand, she understood that graduation meant that Ophelia would lose her entitlement to special education. At that moment, Emma was leaning toward graduation: "This is for her self-esteem. She needs to graduate." Marie had decided the opposite—her son should stay until the end of his entitlement—and was less conflicted:

MARIE: Actually, we were going to push for him to actually—he didn't pass one of the MCAS—to be waived, and they're like, "No, you don't want to do that." I'm like, "Okay . . . you're right." And she said to me very nicely, "What does MCAS mean to Donnie?" I'm like, "Nothing." She says, "But it means a lot in terms of what services he'll receive."

VALERIE: So who gave you the advice?

MARIE: Someone who worked for the state, but you didn't hear it from me. I don't want to get anyone in trouble.

Keeping youths in school could have costs in terms of lost opportunities if they did not receive a high school diploma. Allowing youths to graduate could have costs in terms of lost services.

Parents were also concerned about how the timing of school leaving would affect their families as a whole. Entering the adult service system could mean not just fewer services but less time covered on weekdays. If a family was headed by a single parent or by two parents who both worked, it could cause difficulty for the parents if the young adult was not able to be at home alone safely. They might have to make arrangements for other caregivers at home or cut down their hours or stop working to stay home. It is not unusual for mothers of young children to curtail their employment in order to take care of their children, and mothers of children with disabilities are particularly likely to cut down their hours of employment or stop working altogether to take care of their children, although this is less likely as the children age (Leiter et al. 2004). At a time when most families could count on their children to become more independent, the end of special education services could mean that youths became more dependent upon their families, rather than less. If services and supports were not available, then it would be the families' responsibility to provide any needed care and to find meaningful adult activities for their children. Several parents knew families in which young adults with intellectual disabilities were home all day—sometimes independently, but more often requiring parental supervision.

All in the Timing: The Edge of Adulthood

The stakes are high at this extended boundary between adolescence and adulthood, contested at times, with youths, parents, and schools having different interests that can result in skirmishes around the edges. Youths want to engage in meaningful adult activities in the future, and typically gain important skills during this transition time. Yet those who are more socially aware could find themselves living in limbo and feeling left behind if they realize that their peers have moved on while they have remained. In essence, youths who stay in high school past age eighteen do not have full adult status until they turn twenty-two and are no longer the responsibility of their local school districts. At that time, they finally age out and attain their final marker as adults, finishing high school.

Parents want their children to develop to their maximum potential and to receive all of the services for which they are eligible. They want what is best for their children but also what is best for their families. Given the structure of special education and adult services, their children's "on-time" graduation with their age peers is not always what is best for the children or their families. If youths leave before adult services kick in at age twenty-two, they may not receive adult services. They may also lose resources that they would have access to through the schools. This can be costly to families, especially if parents have to change their labor force participation as a result.

Finally, schools need to fulfill the requirements of special education legislation. Financially, schools would benefit if students left before they aged out. Youths' entitlement to special education beyond the typical age of eighteen was created through special education law at the federal and state levels. Local school districts had no say in the matter and incur additional costs for educating students until they age out because special education is underfunded. School districts do get to determine the content of those additional transition years but receive little guidance about what kind of education they should provide.

Many school districts did their best by the youths in this study. The high schools either developed a program that met their individual needs or placed them out of district in a transition program that did so. These schools focused on work and independent living skills in particular, providing academic courses that stressed practical math and literacy skills and vocational education that moved youths toward the world of work after high school. A few schools were particularly innovative, facilitating concurrent enrollment in local community colleges and developing strong vocational and independent living programs that were immersed in their local communities. The experiences of youths, parents, and professionals related here suggest that while many schools take that responsibility seriously, some fulfill only the letter of the law, warehousing youths or giving them early-bird specials by ensuring that they pass MCAS before they turn twenty-two.

The youths with intellectual disabilities coming of age today have experienced increased educational opportunities as children and adolescents. As a result, they are better prepared to enter into adulthood with daily living and vocational skills that will help them live more independently. Yet they may also face decreased public, community-based supports as adults because of the current economic crisis. Transition from special education to adult service systems at the end of entitlement is not a smooth or easy process for youths and parents. In part, this is because of limited funds for adult services, which may mean a decline in services when youths leave special education. In part, it is because youths and parents find themselves in a new world in which they do not know the rules and are uncertain about the kinds of opportunities that may be available. Leaving high school may be grounds for celebration and for concern.

7

(Im)permanent Markers
of Adulthood

When do individuals become adults? One simple answer is when they turn eighteen, the legal age of majority in the United States. Eighteen-year-olds are allowed to vote, serve in the military, and make legal contracts. A more multifaceted answer is that individuals become adults when they take on adult roles, reaching particular social markers of adulthood, such as completing their schooling, getting a job, living independently, and forming their own families.[1] During the 1950s in the United States, these markers of adulthood were often achieved in an orderly fashion fairly early in adulthood. However, the boundary between adolescence and adulthood has blurred and shifted in recent decades—the pathways to adulthood have changed due to social, cultural, and economic changes in U.S. society (Hogan and Astone 1986; Marini 1984; Modell 1989). Broad changes in the economy and in social norms appear to be contributing to the development of a new phase in the life course called "early" or "emerging" adulthood, in which some markers are attained while others, especially those around family formation, are postponed (Arnett 1998, 2000, 2004; Furstenberg et al. 2003, 2004; Hamilton and Hamilton 2006; Tanner 2006). Economic constraints have made it more difficult for young adults to achieve economic self-sufficiency, and changes in social norms have made it more acceptable for them to reach these markers later in life. (Most of us know people in their twenties who are living with their parents.) It has also become more acceptable to forgo some markers, particularly around family formation.[2]

There is greater awareness now that young people's coming of age experiences differ, depending upon their gender, race and ethnicity, class, religion, nationality, and sexual orientation (Arnett 2003; Nelson 2003; Nelson and McNamara Barry 2005; Nelson et al. 2007). Yet youths with disabilities are almost invisible in the research about transition to adulthood.[3] As noted in chapter 1, as a group they lag behind their peers in terms of completing the traditional markers of adulthood, although they have made strong gains in the past few decades. Existing studies of transition to adulthood among youths with disabilities focus on their attainment of the traditional markers of adulthood, not their understanding of what it means to become an adult. This chapter advances our understanding of how youths with disabilities think about and experience the transition to adulthood in two ways: it emphasizes the qualities that youths with disabilities think differentiate adults from children and examines critically the traditional and subjective markers that they consider necessary in the transition to adulthood, by type of disability. It also includes parents' wishes for their children's young adulthood and some transition difficulties that parents anticipate.

How Do Adults and Kids Differ?

We started our conversations about adulthood with youths by asking them an open-ended question: "People have different ideas about what it means to be an adult. What do you think makes adults different from kids?" Youths identified two key differences: adults have more maturity and responsibility, and they have more power and privileges.

Maturity and Responsibility

Almost all the youths stated in a matter-of-fact way that there were fundamental differences between adults and kids in terms of maturity and responsibility. Derek said: "I think adults are more mature than kids," and Joseph pointed to "maturity, . . . able to decide what's the right thing to do. . . . Kids, on the other hand, they don't have the same ability to determine." Alan, who was twenty and had an intellectual disability, did not yet consider himself an adult. To maturity, he added that adults are "generous, really. They're always there for you." Anna attributed adults' greater maturity to knowledge from life experience: "I guess adults have a better knowledge about how to handle things and stuff. . . . Well, they probably have a better sense of how to deal with problems." Maturity and responsibility were discussed together by many youths, as entangled ideas. Damien explained that "adults are probably different from kids because they might think in a more mature way because when they change their life and go to live on their own, they have more responsibilities. . . . Like, if you're on your own, you have to do it all yourself and everything and make your own choices, and it can be hard sometimes. I mean, it's not like the choice [is] you're at Stop 'n' Shop and should I get wheat or white."

Adults were viewed as accountable for their decisions and actions. They were described as having jobs, paying taxes, and owning homes. Emily explained that "kids kind of can say, 'Okay, I need twenty dollars,' and that's fine for them. But adults have to make that twenty dollars. So it's just different rules." Likewise, Ophelia described adults as "just being responsible and able to take care of yourself, obviously." Youths often framed responsibility in terms of economic self-sufficiency, and also as self-reliance more generally. Kaiser described adults as "responsible" and kids as relying "on their parents for things, and they're more dependent, while adults . . . they rely on themselves more." Frankie explained that "us adolescents, we need to become adults, face the world as if you were an adult. I know that we're not, but I just think that you need to have that sense of responsibility and not be, like, 'I'm only a kid.'" Ted thought that adults "get to make a lot more choices, but those choices also become a huge amount of responsibility," and Carl felt that adults had "the responsibility of knowing what to do, when to do it, and ultimately what not to do."

Adults were seen as able to make better decisions as a result of their accumulated life experiences—a kind of wisdom arose from being older. Kevin felt that it was life experience that really differentiated adults from kids—that, and the responsibilities that they carried. In contrast, the youths thought kids did not always think through their actions. Grace said that "kids are known to be more rebellious and like out of control. Not like out of control, but what's the word? Impulsive, kind of. [Adults are] balanced, maybe, and, like, they had more experience so they're a bit wise, I guess, with situations and decisions." Learning experiences could be both positive and negative. Thomas had gotten into trouble with some friends recently, although apparently he did not pay the same consequences they did. He explained: "Kids—we don't think. We just do things. [*Laughs.*] Like, my friends, the other day—I shouldn't be telling you this, but we were stealing. And the cops came and my friends got caught. And I said, 'Whoa, I didn't expect that to happen.'" Thomas's story suggests that wisdom can come from learning from mistakes, both our own and others.'

Most youths split kids and adults into separate categories in these descriptions, describing adults as mature and responsible, and kids as lacking those qualities. Compared with adults, kids were incompletely developed because of their relative lack of experience and judgment. Four youths described the maturity differences between adults and kids as being more continuous or complex. Sandy and Frederick commented that they were attaining more adultlike awareness as they grew older. Sandy admitted that adults were "wiser for the most part. For instance, as kids you don't have as much knowledge about sexuality or what's to be expected of you when you are older. Also, I think that I'm able to empathize more as I get older, so I'm quite capable of being able to understand where other people are coming from, which is a very useful skill." Frederick felt that adults "simply have a lot more shit on their plates to deal with. Because they obviously have to not only deal with a lot more issues, but they have to deal with the reality of it all, which is something that kids obviously don't deal with because they simply don't know about it. Or more often than not, their minds aren't physically capable of grasping such concepts. Again, I'm one of those people who can, but I'm well aware that most people can't." Frederick saw himself as developing these capabilities during adolescence.

Adolescents could also possess such adult qualities, and adults did not possess them automatically by virtue of their age. As Ted acknowledged: "There are some people who are sixty years old and act like two-year-olds. I mean, it really depends." Adults were not necessarily completely independent, self-sufficient individuals, either. Contrary to most youths, who felt that being responsible meant being wholly responsible for themselves, Elaine separated out being responsible from being entirely independent from others: "For instance, my dad is obviously not an adult just because he has to rely on people. So I think that it's being able to understand that even though you get to rely on yourself, that's also a privilege. And sometimes it's more than okay to ask for help, like in *It's a Wonderful Life*, where everybody's all like, 'You should have asked us for help! We would have helped you! Let us help you!'" Elaine understood that although adults were responsible, sometimes situations arose in which they needed to turn to other people for assistance. Asking for help, being dependent upon others, could be the more responsible path at times, in her view.

Power and Privileges

Adulthood could bring privileges that youths saw as attractive. Steve said: "Adults can drive!"—an activity that many youths yearned to do. Being allowed to drink was mentioned by several, including Jessica: "It could be because adults get more things than kids, and they get different things, like they get to gamble, they get to like play cards and drink, and kids can't." Missy commented that adults could "go to bed whenever they want, and kids have to go to bed at a certain time, because they have to get up in the morning for school, or for day care or for camp or whatever they have to go to for the day." Coleman mentioned that adults can sleep wherever they like; only once had his parents allowed him to stay at his girlfriend's house for the weekend. To these youths, adulthood meant the freedom to engage in adult activities.

Adulthood could also bring power, particularly power over children. Sergeant felt that kids could "not boss people around" like adults could, and Katherine thought that "people listen to adults." Mika described power dynamics that she had once faced at school, which gave her little choice in decisions about her life: "So I think that's a big key factor in that you're able to make decisions that you can apply to, that you want to apply, not decisions that are forced where they're like, 'You're going into this [program] that [a school] is offering, whether you want to go or not.' And I'm like, 'But I've already been like five times.' And they're like, 'Learn it again.' Where [when you're an adult,] you can say, 'Screw the [program],' you know?" Power is held entirely in adult hands, according to these youths' accounts: adults could tell other people what do to, and other people would listen to them. Conversely, youths were told what to do, and other people would not always listen to their desires and views.

Steve articulated a slightly messier power dynamic between adults and kids: "[Adults] have different things that they say, . . . that they think their children are always wrong, and the children think they're right. So it's a kind of a power struggle." In this instance, Steve doesn't specify who wins in the power struggle but shows his awareness that it exists. Mary, who was over eighteen and had an intellectual disability, faced an even more complicated adult-child power dynamic in her work at a preschool. As a teacher, she was one of the adults who was supposed to supervise the children, but she did not feel comfortable in that role when children were "running around and goofing off": "It's very hard for me, because I let the other guys be the teachers. . . . It's really, really hard for me to make them [the children] stop. The rest of the guys will stop them." Mary was expected to use her power in an adult role to get the children to behave, but she experienced difficulty taking that power and using it. Even though she was an adult in terms of both chronological age and the teacher role, she felt uncomfortable using power in that adult role.

Markers of Adulthood

Besides asking youths' opinions about what differentiates adults from kids, we asked them about whether fourteen specific markers were necessary to become an adult. We used benchmarks developed by Jeffrey Arnett, who has spearheaded efforts to broaden our ideas about the markers necessary to achieve adulthood (Arnett 1997, 1998). Arnett includes traditional markers of adulthood, such as reaching age eighteen, finishing education, and no longer living with parents, but also adds more subjective criteria, such as learning to have good control over one's emotions, accepting responsibility for the consequences of one's actions, and deciding on personal beliefs and values independently of parents or other influences. The markers we asked about thus include both objective and subjective criteria, organized here into four general categories: independence, role transitions, chronological transitions, and emotional markers.

The percentage of youths in this study who agreed that each criterion is necessary for adulthood is provided in table 7.1, by type of disability.[4] Youths were included in these questions to the greatest extent possible, and information is provided here from thirty-nine of the fifty-two youths.[5] Once youths decided whether or not a criterion was necessary for adulthood, they were encouraged to elaborate about what each marker of adulthood meant to them.

TABLE 7.1

Youths' Endorsement of Markers of Transition to Adulthood, by Type of Disability (in percent)

	Intellectual (n = 13)	Hidden (n = 17)	Physical/ Sensory (n = 9)	Total (n = 39)
Independence				
Establish equal relationship with parents	69	56	33	55
Be financially independent of parents	85	77	56	74
Live away from parents' household	62	53	22	49
Accept responsibility for consequences of actions	85	88	89	87
Decide on personal beliefs and values independently	69	82	56	77
Role transitions				
Complete education	77	47	22	51*
Marry	31	6	0	13
Have at least one child	46	12	0	20*
Settle into a long-term career	69	35	22	44
Chronological transitions				
Obtain driver's license	62	18	22	33*
Reach age eighteen	62	29	56	46
Emotional transitions				
Commit to long-term love relationship	39	12	0	18*
Maintain good control over your emotions	85	63	78	74
Develop greater consideration for others	92	77	56	77

*p < .05

Independence

Independence markers drew some of the strongest levels of agreement from youth. A majority felt that it was necessary to accept responsibility for the consequences of their actions (87 percent), become financially independent from their parents (74 percent), and decide on personal beliefs and values independently (72 percent). There was much more ambivalence about two other markers of independence, establishing an equal relationship with parents (55 percent) and living outside their parents' households (49 percent). Responsibility for the consequences of actions was key for Frankie: "As an adult, you assume that you are—you do what you want, but be prepared for the aftermath of whatever you do, whether it be a positive thing you do and you win the Nobel Peace Prize, or you go out and get drunk and hit somebody. And I don't think it's very adult to say, 'Oops, I didn't mean it. I only had two drinks.'"

Youths commented on financial independence and living outside their parents' homes more than any of the other independence criteria. They felt that financial independence was crucial. Ted made a distinction between being an adult "legally" (being over the age of eighteen) and acting like an adult: "I'd say if you're adult, you're responsible for your own income. And if you're still living off your parents, you're legally considered an adult, but you're doing something you should have prepared for." Likewise, Steve felt that adults needed to think through their financial situation more carefully once they were on their own: "I think if you're going off to college, you should be somewhat financially independent, so yeah. Even though some people do it, you can't call on your parents every week and say, 'I ran out of money because I went out with my friends too much and now I'm broke. Send me a thousand dollars!'" Frankie stated that "it's important to be able to stand on your own two feet [financially]."

Residential independence was more negotiable as a marker of adulthood, depending upon individual circumstances. Youths thought that it was generally acceptable for young adults to remain in their parents' homes during their twenties, but there was less tolerance for living at home as people grew older. Living with parents during college was definitely acceptable, in Steve's view: "Some people who go to college still have to live with their parents. Well, I'm probably going to end up living with my parents during college, because if you don't live on campus, you really have nowhere else to live." In part, Steve was not sure that he would be able to get the personal care assistance he would need to be able to live on campus with his physical disability. The second part of Steve's answer, "But I kind of want to be home," reflected that he didn't really want to move out of his parents' home quite yet.

Elaine felt that it was not unusual for young adults to live with their parents and disagreed with this criterion for adulthood for that reason: "In my opinion, I would say no, because there are many people who fall back on their parents. And I know it can be very difficult sometimes." Damien explained: "My cousin John, he moved into an apartment or something not long ago, but before that he was still living at my auntie Melissa's house. But he still had a job, he paid for his own stuff, and he paid for his car and everything. He paid taxes, I think, and I think they even might have made him pay room and board. . . . I mean you could still live with your parents and still take care of yourself."

There was no clear consensus about the specific age at which individuals should leave their parents' homes. Ted said: "I guess I'd say like really in your mid-twenties, you really should try to find a place of your own. If you must live with your parents for whatever reason, you should be working regularly, you should be doing things around the house, you should be getting up at the time of an adult, you should be doing the errands if you have a license. You should be doing everything you would do, and you should really try to live alone. If there's some reason you just can't live alone, then you should really, really try to be as independent as you can. . . . See, I really don't think—I really just don't think [living with your parents is] the adult thing to do." Ted insists here that people who are living at home past their midtwenties shouldn't just be independent, they should be full contributing members of their parents' household. They should not only contribute financially, but also do their share of household tasks.

For some youths, living outside of their parents' households was not a requirement for adulthood at any age. Anna explained: "I would say no, because my aunt still lives in her parents' house." Justin felt that "if you're a forty-year-old teacher who teaches twelfth grade and you live at home, that's—that's just kind of creepy. But I don't think that means you're any less of an adult than someone who lives on their own." Sandy also disagreed with this marker of adulthood: "In my opinion, I would say no, because there are many people who fall back on their parents. For instance, you have the people who live in their mothers' basements until they're like forty. And you've also got your richer families who—they rely on their parents for money and things because they just don't care." In these accounts, youths considered people in their forties to definitely be adults, and living at home did not erase the adulthood that came with four decades of life.

Barriers to living independently could keep people living in their parents' households even if they wanted to move out on their own. Frankie explained that some adults still live at home "because maybe their situation doesn't allow them to [live independently]." Frankie would need personal care attendants to assist him with mobility issues if he moved out of his parents' home. Although he might be financially secure, there were other considerations regarding independent living arrangements. And Alan, who had an intellectual disability, wasn't sure when he would be able to move out and live separately from his parents: "I believe eventually, yes. I will have to move out of this house eventually. It would look really bad if I didn't." But it wasn't entirely clear to him how or when he could move toward living in his own home.

Role Transitions

In these youths' parents' generation, traditional role transitions were largely taken for granted: youths then finished their education, settled into a career, got married, and had children. Now many youths see these traditional role transitions as options, as life choices. These markers are no longer necessary for passage into adulthood, although they may occur during adulthood. Just over half felt that it was necessary to finish one's education to become an adult (51 percent), with significant differences by type of disability. Most youths with intellectual disabilities (77 percent) felt that it was necessary, compared with 47 percent of youths with hidden disabilities and 22 percent with physical or sensory disabilities. Youths with intellectual disabilities were significantly more likely to agree with this marker because none of them had yet left high school, even though they were all at least twenty years old. In contrast, their age peers at school had all left. Sean, for example, graduated with his peers but was staying at his local high school until his twenty-second birthday. He could not wait to finish school and start working full-time. His mother explained that "he feels like he's too old for school." Sarah also could not wait to leave her high school: "I have, um, do the graduation. Yeah, graduation next May. [Transition program] graduation. In the gym, graduation and something. Go 'bye.'" According to her mother and father, Sarah didn't quite understand why she was still in school when her age peers had all left. She complained about being there with a common refrain: "I'm eighteen. I can do it myself." Beth also was eager to graduate, after seeing both her brothers graduate from high school and college. Her mother, Jane, said: "They did a very nice graduation ceremony. She had a cap and gown. And it was really good, so she enjoyed that." For youths with intellectual disabilities, finishing high school was a key marker in the transition to adulthood, one they were eager to finally accomplish. Youths with other disabilities were more likely to take this rite of passage for granted, and to view it as separate from becoming an adult.

Just under half the youths felt that it was necessary to settle into a long-term career (44 percent) to achieve adulthood. Ted felt that it was employment itself that was crucial, not necessarily making a commitment to a specific career.

TED: I mean, you can switch around if you want. I'd say it's fine to, if you want to become a policeman for five years and then you want to do something else for ten years, and then a doctor for thirty years, that's fine.

LEXIE: So it's more as long as you have a job?

TED: As long as you have a job, it's fine. As long as you can support yourself, that's all it really comes down to.

Damien felt the same way: "You don't really need to have a career but maybe a job. You could probably work at the McDonald's down the street, you don't have to work at some big company."

Getting married (13 percent) and having at least one child (20 percent) garnered few votes as necessary criteria for adulthood. Most youths simply scoffed at these markers or were surprised to be asked about family formation at their age. These markers were not relevant to their current lives, or to the lives that they planned for the next decade or so. Once again, there is a significant difference by type of disability. Youths with intellectual disabilities were significantly more likely to say that having at least one child was necessary for adulthood (46 percent), compared with two youths (12 percent) with hidden disabilities and none of the youths with physical disabilities. Several youths with intellectual disabilities specifically stated that they wanted to have children as a life goal, while none of the youths with other disabilities stated this as a goal. For example, one of Alan's life goals, according to both him and his mother, was to adopt children when he was older. Youths with intellectual disabilities were more likely to emphasize family formation markers as important to entering adulthood, whether it was being committed to a long-term love relationship, getting married, or having children. These markers held little relevance for youths with physical or hidden disabilities, much like their age peers without disabilities (Arnett 1997, 2001).

Chronological Transitions

Not even half the youths felt that reaching age eighteen was necessary for becoming an adult (46 percent). Donnie was an exception: "Yeah, definitely, because once you reach the age of eighteen, you are full, you are fully recognized as an adult." Mika was also matter-of-fact about the age of majority, saying that it is "obvious" that turning eighteen makes people adults, and that "it's proved, the laws have proved it." Yet several youths with physical and hidden disabilities were particularly critical of the idea that turning eighteen made people adults. Frankie said that "everybody walks to their own beat," indicating that the eighteen-year-old cutoff was too rigid as a marker of adulthood. Damien explained that "sometimes you may be the age of eighteen but your maturity may not be up there, or either that, or may be over that, and may have come earlier than eighteen." Similarly, Justin explained that "in the eyes of the law," being eighteen makes you an adult, "but I don't think that means you're mature." Sandy thought that in some cases being eighteen could make someone an adult, "but, for instance, I consider myself very close to adult, because I think like one. Some people mature much faster than others. It could be that technically you're still teens. . . . I'll have to go with no on that one." Coleman felt that it wasn't the number of years someone had been alive that was important. Instead, it was "the experience, mental preparation, and just how ready you are for actually going out there." Someone could be very mature, based upon his or her accomplishments or ability to make good judgments, but be under eighteen. Hermione said: "If somebody is really mature, like there are people who become independent early, like they live on their own, so I guess they can be considered adults maybe."

Coleman had bumped up against what he saw as artificial age requirements for the purchasing of video games: "There has been this whole controversy of, oh, you have to be eighteen to buy it, you have to be seventeen. And I kind of think, well, I was seventeen when I bought Resident Evil, but say I was only able when I was eighteen, well, am I mentally prepared for it? I believe I am. Do I know that it is a game and that it's not real life? Yes. Do I know not to shoot anybody? Yes. It's just kind of almost that common sense that comes along with adulthood that I believe makes an adult." Frederick was the most critical in his response to this marker of adulthood, calling the turning-eighteen phenomenon a "cultural pretense," explaining that it was a "culturally revered transitional period" made up by our culture.

Only 33 percent of youths agreed that having a driver's license was necessary for becoming an adult. Frederick, who agreed with this criterion, said that a driver's license "doubles as an ID. So, if anything, it does quite literally serve as proof of your existence if not your being an adult." The relatively low percentage of youths who thought that having a driver's license was necessary for adulthood did not mean that youths thought having a driver's license was unimportant, however. It just wasn't a requirement for adulthood. A driver's license represented freedom and accessibility. Steve explained: "Yeah, because you can't be thirty-five and asking your mom to drive you around everywhere. 'I want to go to the bar with my friends! Drive me!' . . . 'Yes, honey, but you have to be in bed before twelve.'" Hermione was aware that she "should" have had her driver's license already but did not: "That's a sensitive talk with me. I just have my learner's permit. I didn't—there are a few reasons I didn't take—I'm just finishing driver's ed now and so I just had to recently renew my learner's permit because I had it for so long that it expired. So I don't have my license yet and that sort of bothers me." When she was asked if she planned to get her license, she replied, "I hope so."

Youths with intellectual disabilities were significantly more likely to state that having a driver's license was necessary for adulthood (62 percent), compared with youths with physical and sensory disabilities (22 percent) and those with hidden disabilities (18 percent). Youths with intellectual disabilities could not take this marker of adulthood for granted because in some instances they knew that they would have substantial difficulty passing the written and driving tests to get their licenses. Donnie, who had an intellectual disability and was over age eighteen, said: "I don't have a driver's license, so—it is going to be very hard for me to get around. So if I want to go for my driver's license—oh, man." Alan's dream job involved cars—he loved cars, antique cars especially, and wanted a job that had something, anything, to do with them. Alan explained that he had tried to take his driving test once but got anxious and left. Alan's mother had heard that there was testing through a hospital for youths with disabilities and thought that he might want to try the alternative test. She wanted him to succeed and said: "I think he can, I really do. But he gets upset with me because he thinks I'm saying he can't do something."

Sarah desperately wanted to be able to drive: "I need a car. Me mom buy a car. I need car and keys. I have my own car with radio. Listen to the radio. [*Makes musical noises.*] I wanna drive. Drive. Just drive. Easy. I drive easy with a cell phone." Sarah's parents understood her desire to drive and tried to explain to her the steps that were needed to achieve that goal. Her mother said: "My son is sixteen and he got his license and he drives his own car, and [Sarah] keeps saying she wants to drive and she wants a car. So that part's kind of difficult. But we tell her, 'Maybe someday you'll get your license.' I say, 'Sarah, you have to read the book and pass the test. If you go get that book and read it and pass, fine.' She'll say, 'Never mind, maybe when I'm [older].'" Mary's life goals also included driving. She wanted to get married, have a family, and drive a red car. Her intellectual disability made the car goal difficult. Her mother said: "We have told her we'll do everything we can to support her getting her license, but there are certain minimal things she has to be able to do. So we have a plan for how we could make that happen. It starts with her passing, of course, the driver's permit exam. I'm not sure that she can do that." If Mary did pass the exam, her parents planned to get her a golf cart so that she could practice around their neighborhood and perhaps eventually get her license. Clearly this is not practical for many families, due to their economic situations and neighborhoods, but it demonstrates Mary's parents' commitment to help her achieve her goals in life.

Emotional Markers

A majority of youths agreed that two of the emotional criteria were necessary for adulthood: maintaining good control over emotions (74 percent) and developing greater consideration for others (77 percent). Relatively few felt that it was necessary to be committed to a long-term love relationship (18 percent). Control over emotions was a topic that struck a nerve with several youth. Neither Hermione nor Kevin thought that good control over emotions was necessary for adulthood. Kevin thought that if you always needed to have good control over your emotions, "then no one's an adult." And Hermione explained: "No, I mean that would be a robot, not an adult. It's good to be pretty controlled. But occasionally if something really upsetting happens, it's only human to react." Justin saw this issue very differently: "Let me give you an example. I was at the urologist and she told me all this [about my health] and I wanted to flip out and scream and cry and yell, but I didn't. I just asked the appropriate questions, that I thought were appropriate. Then when I left I just, I went into the bathroom, looked in the mirror and took a deep breath and said, 'Wow, this is really happening.' I called one of my friends and I talked to him for a while. But I think if I had flipped out they would have been like, 'Wow, this kid is psychologically disturbed.' I'm certain if I flipped out they would have called security on me and had me escorted from the building. So I do think that you have to be under control of your emotions." He felt that his calm response to bad health news was a clear indicator that he was adult enough to be in charge of his own life, and expressed pride in how he handled that difficult encounter.

Of the three emotional markers, only being committed to a long-term love relationship received low marks as an indicator of adulthood. Here we see an interesting difference again by type of disability. No youths with physical disabilities agreed with this marker, and only two youths with hidden disabilities agreed (12 percent). Frankie, who had a physical disability, disagreed "because some people never get married, and they're still—they still, I think that it's kind of naïve to think that way. I'm very open-minded, so I try to consider all people's lives and how we're all different and we all come from different situations, are brought up differently, so. . . . There are so many different facets of somebody's life that people too often judge by what society says is right. Like society says that gay people can't marry."

Most youths with intellectual disabilities did not think that this marker needed to be met for an individual to be an adult. Chico was clear about this: "Oh, no, no, it's not necessary. Well, that's what most people do, but it's not necessary." However, compared to youths with other disabilities, those with intellectual disabilities were significantly more likely to say that being committed to a long-term relationship was a criterion for adulthood. Five out of thirteen youths with intellectual disabilities (39 percent) did agree, including Sarah.

SARAH: I have a boyfriend. I have Alex.

LEXIE: Oh, you do?

SARAH: Uh huh. My Alex go to prom. Prom is on the eighteenth. . . . We'll have a house and me and Alex will have a house. . . . Me and Alex have a drink and then me and Alex have a friends together and me and Alex have older and me and Alex talk together. Me and Alex go out. Dinner or something.

Sarah saw her relationship with Alex as making her an adult, and her life plans after high school centered partly on her anticipated shared life with Alex. The youths with intellectual disabilities who did agree with this criterion felt consistently that attaining family goals was central to their becoming adults.

Looking back across these criteria, two key patterns stand out: there is a high level of agreement with many of the independence and emotional markers of adulthood, and key differences in opinion between youths with intellectual disabilities and youths with other disabilities. The items that received the most support included one objective marker of adulthood, financial independence from parents, while the rest were more subjective in nature: accepting responsibility for the consequences of actions, maintaining good control over emotions, and developing greater consideration for others. Chronological transitions and traditional role transitions received much less support. Subjective markers of adulthood are important for the youths with disabilities here, just as they are for youths in the general U.S. population (Arnett 1997, 2001).

Parents' Expectations for Their Children's Young Adulthood

The parents in this study came of age when the traditional markers of adulthood were typically achieved in an orderly fashion. Becoming an

adult meant attaining those markers, starting with finishing their education and getting a job, and then becoming more independent both socially
and financially from their parents. As I have noted, the transition to adulthood is no longer so tidy. What are parents' current expectations of their
children's transition to adulthood? I asked parents to "imagine [your child]
when s/he is twenty-five years old. What would you like his/her life to be
like then?"

Parents sometimes wished for their children to achieve traditional
markers of adulthood, especially finishing their education (22 percent)
and being employed (44 percent). But by far the most common goal was
to have their child living independently by age twenty-five: 62 percent
mentioned this. A small but vocal minority of parents (16 percent) also
mentioned their children's personal lives, such as having a boyfriend or
girlfriend, getting married, or having children. Typically, parents envisioned a kind of package deal, combining independent living with one or
two of the other educational, employment, or romantic goals. Celie, whose
son Frankie had a physical disability, said that by age twenty-five, "I'd like
him to be independent and living on his own, or with his partner or wife,
or whatever that is. [*Laughs.*] Hopefully be gainfully employed doing something he loves to do." Rita, whose son Steve also had a physical disability,
said: "I'd like him to be well educated. And independent, both physically
with less assistance from family or PCA [personal care attendant], and
financially independent. Either living in an apartment with someone else,
or possibly married. I have the same goals as I see for his brother." Both
Celie and Rita commented on their sons' ability to live independently—all
the parents of youths with physical or sensory disabilities mentioned this
as an important goal that they'd like their children to achieve by the age of
twenty-five, most indicating that they expected it to occur. In contrast,
only half the parents of youths with hidden disabilities mentioned independent living as a goal, and they had little to say about it—their com-
ments focused more on their children's educational and employment
goals (finishing college and finding jobs).

Almost all the parents of youths with intellectual disabilities mentioned independent living as a key goal but voiced mixed feelings about
their children moving out of their homes. On the one hand, parents typically expected their children to move out at some point, just as they would

expect any child to do once they were old enough. On the other hand, it could be difficult for parents to think about how to help their children get from where they currently were in life to the independent life that their parents envisioned for them. Reva and J.J. talked about what they wanted for their son Chico's life:

REVA: To be as normal as it can be, to get a job, to be able to take care of himself.

J.J.: Be part of society.

REVA: Be part of society, yeah.

J.J.: When he was three years old, we could not imagine ten years, or even twelve, or even sixteen, what it would be like, given his disability where we was at that age, and we had no idea where he's going to turn out. We still don't know where he's going to turn out, because—

REVA: Maturity.

J.J.: Maturity is changing, he's developing late, delayed development. . . .

REVA: I want him to get married, have kids, and be successful. But my main thing is for him to be happy and functional.

J.J.: And out of the house.

REVA: No, he can stay as long as he wants.

[*Laughter.*]

J.J.: That's why you get a difference.

Parents of youths with intellectual disabilities often worried about their children living elsewhere, outside their supervision and care. As a result, these parents defined "independent living" more broadly than did the other parents, as their child not living at home with them. Living independently could mean living in a group home or in a supervised apartment shared with other adults with intellectual disabilities, ideally with people of their own gender and age. It rarely meant that the youths would live alone, unsupervised—that would be unsafe for many of the youths with intellectual disabilities. More scaffolding was needed to create living situations in which young adults with intellectual disabilities might succeed. Jane would like her daughter Beth, who had autism, "to be able to live in her own home. That may be a shared living or a group home, I don't—I mean, there's many options that I'm just starting to hear about. And finding out what she's eligible for is another story. But to be in a home with other women her own age, you know, maybe two or three, not many. She likes to be in a smaller group. I do know she needs twenty-four-hour supervision. So it would have to be somewhere with a live-in situation." Jane was hoping that the Massachusetts DDS would fund Beth's living situation, but acknowledged that it was unlikely to happen anytime soon. DDS sorted people who were eligible for adult services based on their disability-related and family-based needs. As an intact, two-parent family, Jane said, they were not a priority and Beth would be unlikely to receive residential services soon. Joan and Patrick faced a similar situation—they wanted their son Brent to have the choice between living at home or in a group home funded by DDS but knew that Brent was unlikely to receive residential services unless there was what Joan called "some kind of a catastrophe." Patrick agreed: "Right, if we both died at once." And Joan added: "They seem to wait for some kind of crisis thing."

In response to the lack of housing opportunities through DDS, several families were developing do-it-yourself approaches to facilitating their children's transition to independent living. Families with fewer resources tried to do this on the cheap. Kelsey planned to help her niece Kayla: "Right now our short-term goal is that when she turns twenty-two that we have a place for her to move into with a roommate. Basically, I don't want to put her with someone who is severely handicapped, but handicapped enough for her to have a staff person. . . . But if she gets a roommate who is, then she could survive. . . . That's one of our goals. We're talking about buying a house or a trailer so that she would have a place to live. A little more hands-on versus handing her off to an agency. I don't like the idea of handing her off to an agency." Kelsey and her family did not have many financial resources but felt that they could swing buying a trailer for Kayla and were hoping to find someone else who had staffing from DDS to share it—they would provide the housing and the other person would provide the staffing. Kayla didn't need much supervision but did need some.

Angela's family had many more resources to devote to their son William's departure from the family nest. They had just purchased a house and were working with several other families whose children were also about to turn twenty-two, and with an agency, Toward Independent Living and Learning, which provided technical assistance to set up the housing, Angela said: "So, at about twenty-five, my hope—I think I can speak for my husband—is that [William] would be living comfortably in a group of peers, very close to us, but independently from us so that he has his own door key, his own plan for the week, and he can kind of shut us out, if you will, with that life of his better without parents hovering or being close. But he has more of a choice about when family is inside his life and when the family is just waiting to be invited. So that's important to us." Angela and her husband had started this arrangement and recruited other families to join them—they were pooling their collective resources to pay for and staff the housing to support their children independently. This arrangement came at a high cost, however—Angela estimated that it would be about $40,000 per year. A few other families had heard about these plans and were trying to pool their meager resources to make similar arrangements. Most of these arrangements were more along the lines of Kelsey's plans to buy a trailer for Kayla—one youth teased his mother that she was going to have him live out in a shed.

Most parents knew that their children with intellectual disabilities would likely live with them into the near future. Norma, a professional who had a daughter with a disability, understood that young adults in their twenties were more likely to live with their parents in general but felt that the situations were not entirely comparable: "I have people say to me, 'I've got three kids, and they all came home after college because they—.' But that's different. That's different. They can still leave whenever they want, because they're ready to. They're just trying to have a little more money in their pockets. So it's really hard to compare them to the students that we're talking about, I think. But that's a very motherly point of view." For some youths with disabilities, especially those with intellectual disabilities, living at home may be a more long-term arrangement if other resources are not available to help them get by without their parents.

(Im)permanent Markers

Individuals in families lead interdependent lives (Elder 1991), and young adults in the United States in general today are prolonging their residential and financial dependence on their families as an adaptive strategy (Aquilino 1999). Youths with disabilities are more likely than youths without disabilities to experience constraints, which include the same kinds of economic constraints but also perhaps care-related constraints, depending on the nature of their disabilities.

Subjective markers of adulthood are important in the lives of all youths who are coming of age in contemporary U.S. society. In part, these markers may receive the highest levels of agreement among youths with disabilities because they may be more attainable on the cusp of adulthood compared with some of the traditional markers of adulthood. Accepting responsibility for the consequences of our actions or developing greater consideration for others do not depend on anyone's economic circumstances. In part, these markers also capture ways in which these youths begin to think and act in ways that they perceive to be more adult, particularly in their social interactions. The youths here believed that what really differentiated adults from children was that adults were more mature and responsible than children, and had more power and privileges. These subjective definitions of adulthood highlight some of the subtler building blocks of adult identity.

8

Missing Links

Today, the transition to adulthood is receiving a great deal of attention.[1] Yet if we look across the entire life course, that transition is only one of many. The transition from home to preschool has become a common experience. The transition from home or preschool to kindergarten. Depending on the school system, the transition to middle school or junior high school. Then high school, with various exits—dropping out, getting a certificate, getting a diploma, or aging out. That's three to five transitions before youths reach adulthood, when many more follow. Why all the attention to the transition to adulthood now? Part of it is fueled by concerns that youths in the United States in general are not transitioning as early or as smoothly as in the past. And youths with disabilities lag behind their peers in terms of attainment of traditional markers of adulthood. They are making strides as a group and are increasingly likely to complete high school and enter college compared with youths who came of age several decades ago. However, there is still room for progress.

Transition to adulthood is one of those moments in an individual's life where knowledge and systems of support can make a difference, having ripple effects across the rest of the life course, "the universal escalator on which everyone rides."[2] Some rides are smoother than others, and youths may get on and off the escalator at different places, with different results. Therefore, more effort is being put into launching youths with disabilities into adulthood, with the goal of improving their personal and financial prospects. Amanda, a professional who had an adult child with a disability, described life as a chain: "You have a chain, a beautiful chain. It takes all those little nuts and bolts that are wired together to show the beauty of what you're wearing. One missing, it's not a chain. You can just let it drop. It's going to sit on the side of your neck. It's not going to stay on your neck. It's that missing one. It doesn't have to be two, three broken ones. Just one missing, it's not a chain anymore. You have to make it, you have to keep it connected, with knowledge. Basic knowledge, someone just knowing what to do, where to go."

The link between adolescence and adulthood is one of the vulnerable links in the chain of the life course. Amanda had a frustrating experience trying to get adult services for her son from DDS, and after being put off multiple times over a sixteen-month period, resorted to writing to Senator Edward Kennedy's office to advocate on her son's behalf. His office forwarded her letter to DDS. Everything turned out fine in the end, but this experience made her aware of the vulnerability of the link between high school and adult disability systems, and the role that parents may have to play in creating that link through knowledge and advocacy.

Disability policy over the past few decades has attempted to improve the prospects and opportunities of youths with disabilities, but the youths' and parents' experiences reported in this book demonstrate that there are some missing links between disability policy at the federal level and the lived experiences of youths with disabilities and their parents at the ground level. The Individuals with Disabilities Education Act, the Rehabilitation Act, and the Americans with Disabilities Act are all in place, but youths are not fully informed about them, and the rights those laws confer are not always accessible to youths and their families. A recent report on special education outcomes for youths with disabilities by the U.S. General Accounting Office cited five major problems reported by stakeholders in the transition process. They were: lack of self-advocacy training (with youths as the stakeholders), insufficient information about the transition process (with parents as the stakeholders), absence of linkages between school systems and service providers (with teachers as the stakeholders), lack of vocational education and community work experience (with researchers as the stakeholders), and lack of transportation (with federal, state, and local officials as the stakeholders). In this book, youths and parents have had plenty to say about issues that are relevant to the first three problems mentioned (lack of self-advocacy training, insufficient information, and absence of linkages), and professionals offered recommendations that address these problems directly. Therefore, I focus my recommendations upon those three issues.[3]

Youth Self-Advocacy

A recent mandate in the Individuals with Disabilities Education Act (IDEA) encourages youths' self-advocacy by giving students the right to participate in their Individual Education Plan (IEP) meetings if "a purpose of the meeting will be the consideration of the postsecondary goals for the child and the transition services needed to assist the child in meeting those goals." If the student is unable to attend, then school staff "must take other steps to ensure that the child's preferences and interests are considered" (IDEA §300.321[b]). In this language, Congress gave youths the right to participate in the meetings where decisions are made about their transition services and plans for the future.

This small shift toward greater youth participation is consistent with broader philosophical changes in the disability rehabilitation field. The 1992 Amendments to the Rehabilitation Act, which funds vocational rehabilitation nationwide, mentions self-determination specifically: "Disability is a natural part of the human experience and in no way diminishes the rights of individuals to live independently, enjoy self-determination, make choices, contribute to society, pursue meaningful careers and enjoy full inclusion and integration in the economic, political, social, cultural and educational mainstream of American society" (§2[a][3][A–F]). The statement about self-determination in the amendments has spurred researchers and policy makers to think more about the concept and how it may be implemented (Fenton, Batavia, and Roody 1993; Zimmerman and Warschausky 1998). For example, youth empowerment is included as a component in current Youth Transition Demonstration projects being run by the Social Security Administration with youths who are receiving Supplemental Security Income (SSI) benefits.[4] Several studies have found links between youths' self-determination and the attainment of postsecondary goals, holding out the promise that self-determination will improve adult outcomes (Algozzine et al. 2001; Field and Hoffman 2002; Test et al. 2004; Wehmeyer and Schwartz 1997).

The accounts of youth participation shared in chapter 3 demonstrate that we cannot rely upon annual IEP transition-planning meetings alone to provide youths with self-determination skills. This one small congressional mandate is not sufficient to foster youths' self-advocacy—only a handful of youths in this study were active, empowered participants in their meetings. Some recent work suggests six key dimensions of "critical youth empowerment": "(1) a welcoming, safe environment, (2) meaningful participation and engagement, (3) equitable power-sharing between youth and adults, (4) engagement in critical reflection on interpersonal and sociopolitical processes, (5) participation in sociopolitical processes to affect change, and (6) integrated individual- and community-level empowerment" (Jennings et al. 2006, 32). None of these dimensions were routinely part of IEP transition meetings. The transition-planning process is adult driven and requires little input from youths. Most youths could be described as vessels in those meetings, not as active participants (Wong, Zimmerman, and Parker 2010). Even when youths did participate, their actions were largely symbolic—they had a limited voice without much power when setting agendas or making decisions. Adults had tremendous power in these settings, shaping youths' understandings of their options (Lukes 1974, 23).

Children's and youths' participation has been described as a ladder.[5] At the very bottom, adults manipulate children into carrying the adults' messages. At the very top, children initiate activities themselves: children set up a project and may invite adults to help them make decisions, but adults do not have a guaranteed role.[6] Much of youths' participation in IEP transition meetings was at the third of eight rungs, tokenism. Youths were asked for their views but had little choice in matters. The youths I describe as empowered are at the sixth rung: "adult-initiated, shared decisions with children." At this level, the adults provide the impetus but the youths are included at every step and are involved in making real decisions. The extent and tenor of youths' participation in their IEP transition-planning meetings was shaped by the nature of their disabilities and by their attitudes about their disabilities, but also by the adults around them, who had the power to facilitate or dampen their participation.[7] Adults have the authority to socialize youths into particular roles as the subjects of disability policy. Just as there is a spectrum of youth participation, there is a spectrum of adult facilitation of youth participation. On one end of the spectrum of adult facilitation, adults attempt to convince youths to go along with the decisions that they make for them. At the other end, adults strive to convince and teach youths that they should take a full, active role in making decisions about their futures. This route admittedly requires substantially more effort on the behalf of both adults and youths and has the potential to make the IEP transition-planning process harder for the adults if youths disagree with the decisions that adults would like them to make.

The goal of empowering youths to advocate on their own behalf is to enable them to make their own decisions and take action for themselves, to the greatest degree possible. It is therefore both a means and an end, "a continuing dynamic" (Cornwall 2008, 273). The professionals who were interviewed were entirely supportive of youths having greater voice in the decisions that were being made about their lives. About a third of the professionals explicitly used their interviews to vent about the lack of control they felt that youths had over their lives. Alexandra, a professional in a state agency, said that youths typically were not prepared to work with professionals in her agency when they came out of high school: "I should say, from an adult perspective, from the state agency perspective, that after they leave high school, they come here. Their real life is when they start here. They have to have the ability to make decisions. They have to have the ability to understand and maneuver, and know how agencies work, and how to advocate for themselves. [Otherwise,] how do we work with them? How do we get them to understand what they want to do and then develop a plan with them, and help them follow through with the plan?" It was difficult to work with youths effectively if they were not accustomed to speaking for themselves. Maya, who also worked for a state agency, thought along much the same lines: "So if they learn that from the very beginning, I think that if schools were able to apply that from the very beginning and teach the decision-making skills, or at home teach the decision-making skills, then when they do come to the state agencies, that is something that they'll already know. I think from the state agency point of view, I think the policy of—right now, what we're trying to do is develop like a youth—someone who can work directly with the youth, who will understand that youth are going to leave school without that understanding, without those skills, without those advocacy skills. And then how do we work with them?"

Professionals located some of the responsibility for fostering youths' advocacy skills at school and some at home, but mostly emphasized parents' roles. (Once again, responsibility for change was placed largely upon parents, not upon public systems that serve youths with disabilities.) Several professionals used their interviews as an opportunity to say things that they wished they could say directly to parents. Martin said that one of his greatest challenges was "getting parents to see their kids as adults who live in the world, not disabled adults. A lot of the education is with the parents and not with the kids. . . . They're real people who live in the world. Even though they have a disability, they will still face all the bad things that everyone else does. When they turn twenty-one, they're probably going to get drunk." Adam, a professional in a community-based organization who had a disability, explained: "A lot of times, the parents are used to a certain way of life. They're used to basically making decisions for these kids and stuff like that, but these kids, once again, they want to become independent. I try to help them, different strategies, ways to empower themselves so that they can become the decision makers and be part of the decisions that are being made on their behalf. I hit them with a lot of good advice and stuff like that. I also try to make them aware of the different agencies out here, within our community, that provide services for the disabled community as well."

Megan, also in a community-based organization and a professional who had a disability, wanted parents "to step back and let the child have some room! That's one of the things. I had one parent of a student that's living on her own. Mom was still trying to run her life. And I was like, you got to let her make mistakes. You got to let her live. And that's the whole risk thing. . . . Just letting them—like pushing them forward, but then let them go. Just like you would a regular kid. And everyone's going to make mistakes. And you've got to realize that. I make mistakes every day." Ivan, another professional, thought along much the same lines: "If we never learn to fail, we are never going to be able to have good emotional regulation. [If you've] never practiced failing, you can't regulate yourself because you never experienced those feelings. And so the less frequently they're grown up and having failed experiences, the less ability they will have later in life to deal with them. So you're setting them up for failure. You can't protect your child forever. You're not going to be there forever."

Megan and Ivan both refer to one of the main tenets of the independent living movement: the right to fail. (Other major tenets include consumer control, cross-disability participation, choice, and the exercise of power [Carr n.d.].) Individuals should have the right to take risks and face the consequences of those decisions. Otherwise their growth as individuals is stunted, as others protect them from trying and succeeding or failing on their own. This is a difficult dilemma for all parents, not just those whose children have disabilities. No parent wants their child to be harmed, yet we limit our children's development if we don't let them explore and make their own mistakes. But which mistakes are too serious, resulting in too much harm? This raises an important issue—competency. Competence is often raised in discussions about increasing children's participation in making decisions. There is some concern that while their participation should be encouraged in general, their autonomy in making real decisions should be constrained by their competence and understanding of the available options (Landsdown 1995). From this perspective, youths can be seen as "partial citizens of the present" who will be full citizens upon reaching adulthood (Howe and Covell 2005, 58).

Yet if we take competence as necessary for participation but do not help youths develop competence to participate, we keep their development static. There is clearly a need for some scaffolding here to help youths develop advocacy skills over time, because "even as the 'silence' is broken, the initial demands of the dominated may be vague, ambiguous, partially developed" (Gaventa 1982, 19). Some youths with disabilities may need permanent scaffolding to provide support while maximizing their participation in making decisions. For example, as we saw in chapter 3, Kayla's aunt Kelsey explained that Kayla signs her own IEP, but that she must do so in the presence of an adult who does not work for the school because of her intellectual disability and tendency to defer to people in authority. This procedure allowed Kayla more independence in making decisions while protecting her from being persuaded to sign something that was not in her best interest. Permanent scaffolding is not inconsistent with the tenets of the independent living movement. Irving Zola, a leader in that movement, summed this up: "We in the movement would argue that independence cannot be measured by the mundane physical tasks we can do but by the personal and economic decisions we make. It is not the quantity of tasks we can perform without assistance that matters but the quality of life we can live with help" (Zola 1983, 347). Although Zola's statement is based partly on his experience as an adult with a physical disability, it can fit individuals with other disabilities.

If we think of youths as having evolving capacities, that opens up questions as to how best to facilitate their development of self-advocacy skills. It's easy to point our fingers at parents and say that they should do more to empower their children, but additional knowledge and skills about empowerment need to come from somewhere and parents have largely not been given information about how to help their children develop those skills. The parents who mentored their children's advocacy had simply taken it upon themselves to do so with no guidance at all—they just worked their way through it, feeling that it helped the youths prepare for their futures. For the empowered youths described in chapter 3, parental and professional mentors were crucial—they provided information and support, urging youths to take as much control as possible. A study of successful young adults with disabilities also points out the importance of adults in facilitating youths' participation, calling them benefactors (Powers, Singer, and Todis 1996). Many of the professionals I interviewed described themselves in this light, particularly those who had disabilities. They identified with the youths with whom they worked and wanted to be role models for them. The few youths who managed to find these professionals had benefited from their tutoring—they had much more knowledge than other youths about the adult systems that existed and the range of services that they might expect to receive. Both parents and professionals may serve as mentors and benefactors to youths, helping them to develop advocacy skills.

Alexandra, a professional who had a disability, pointed out the role that youths could play in mentoring other youths. She and some of her colleagues worked with youths to develop leadership skills—not just to advocate for themselves, but to try to create broader social change. They set their sights higher than self-advocacy at the individual level:

> I think the biggest recommendation would be that these politicians
> and the people up in the statehouse are making these laws and stuff
> like that, and they're making these rules and things, and these

systems are supposed to be geared towards the youth. I think it would be better if they let the youth sit in on these proceedings. That way, they can get their perspective and their input on what a youth is. Because, just to be truthful about this, a lot of these people that are making these rules, they have lived two lifetimes already, twenty-five years removed or more from their youth. In a lot of cases, they don't have the slightest idea. They're out of touch with what goes on with today's youth. Because a lot of those laws and stuff and a lot of these systems devised today are geared toward yesterday's youth. People that have old skills and stuff like that. They're not even willing to consider what the youth have to say. You have to involve the youth in this decision making.

Alexandra saw mismatches between disability policy and the lives of the youths with whom she worked. She had experienced such mismatches herself as she moved from high school to college and independent living, and wanted contemporary youths to have the opportunity to address those mismatches through broader civic advocacy on disability and youth policy.

Improving Information

Youths, and especially their parents, struggled to find information that would identify future opportunities for adulthood and help them prepare for their transition. Federal legislation and state policies created rights and opportunities for youths, but it could be hard to find appropriate resources. They were often stealth resources, to be gained only through a great deal of time and effort and conversations with professionals and other parents. Youths relied on their schools somewhat for information, but mostly relied on their parents. Parents relied to some extent on their children's schools but largely didn't trust the schools, especially public schools, to provide them with all the answers. Parents trusted fellow travelers—other parents—and parent resource organizations such as the Federation, Urban Pride, and Viva Urbana. But each of these organizations has its own turf, its own constituency of youths and families. Joan, whose son had an intellectual disability, complained that "the most difficult thing is whether it's the Independent Living Centers, whether it's the Institute for Community Inclusion, whether it's the Federation for Children with Special Needs, they all have different niches and strengths and *they'll* refer you to a place." Each source would send her in a different direction, and it took a lot of time and energy to follow up on all the leads and connect the dots. There was rarely any coordination of information about resources, in her view.

This is a spotty way to collect information, resulting in inequalities in social capital between families and raising questions about why there isn't a more centralized source of information about transition. At the national level, there is a clearinghouse for information on transition through the NICHCY, the National Dissemination Center for Children with Disabilities, which is funded by the U.S. Department of Education. Its website summarizes transition issues, includes quotes from IDEA on students' rights, and provides links to additional details and resources.[8] Yet only one of the families I talked with was aware of this resource, and the website is largely centered on IDEA, which governs what is supposed to happen in high schools. Adult disability services are provided by state agencies, so more state-specific information is needed to help youths and parents see where transition planning should take them after high school. There is a need for information that links federal and state disability policies for youths and their parents. States could provide that link by creating their own websites that connect to the NICHCY website for the federal information, and that describe all the state-level agencies that provide adult disability services and supports and the populations that each serves.

The U.S. General Accounting Office report mentioned earlier identified parents as the stakeholders when describing insufficient information about the transition process as a problem (GAO 2003). I suggest that youths should be stakeholders here as well. I have noted that social capital was distributed unevenly *within* families as well as *between* them, with parents holding more social capital than their children. If youths are to play more active roles in making decisions, then they must have sufficient information to make informed choices. One way in which we could improve youths' access to information about transition would be to foster direct connections between youths and disability advocacy organizations (Tisdall 1994). Here is a place where Independent Living Centers could play an important role—they specialize in knowledge about adult disability resources and always have adults with disabilities on staff. These adults could be role models to youths.

Michele, who worked for a community-based disability organization, also suggested that community-based programs that serve youths in their communities should have disability on their radar and help spread information—they might reach youths who were otherwise not being included in networks of social capital. These community-based programs should identify youths with disabilities and refer them to disability organizations. In this way, youths not included in other networks of information would be identified and served. Michele explained: "I think one of the most important policy changes that could be made is that any agency that receives funding to work with transition-aged youth should be required to have information about transition-aged youth with disabilities. If I'm providing funding to this after-school program to work with kids in this age group, they should be required to know and understand and be able to demonstrate their ability to provide information related to transition for youth with disabilities. . . . It's the only way to bring the issue out of the closet." She had visited a prominent youth community service organization recently to recruit youths for a youth leadership program and told the staff there that the program was open to any youths with an Individual Education Program at school. She was told: "Oh, we don't have any kids with disabilities." This program works with high-risk youths in low-income communities. In Michele's opinion, "they're bound to have kids on IEPs that they're working with," but the staff person there was clear: "No, no, I'm pretty sure we're not working with any kids with disabilities." Michele was frustrated because she knew that these programs had to be serving youths with disabilities but did not want to acknowledge it. In her view, this was a missed opportunity to connect youths with disability-related supports and resources, and she vowed to improve disability awareness in the community.

Building Better Bridges

There are large cracks between high school and adult disability laws and services. One crack, documented in chapter 5, relates to the experiences of youths who were college bound and results from the differences between

IDEA (which is parent driven) and the disability laws that apply to college students, namely Section 504 of the Rehabilitation Act and the Americans with Disabilities Act, both of which require adults to act on their own behalf. Youths and parents were typically not aware that this gap existed until the youths reached college and had to document their disabilities once again for the disability services staff, and then advocate for themselves. Youths and parents were rarely warned that they were starting anew in a different system of rules and regulations. Youths and parents need to be made aware in advance that youths will be on their own regarding the use of adult disability rights when they reach college, and that they and their parents must build their own bridges between high school and college.

Another major gap exists between the services that youths are entitled to under IDEA and the services that they may be eligible for through state disability agencies. In Massachusetts, for example, this gap may affect youths who seek state adult disability services through agencies such as the Department of Developmental Services, the Massachusetts Rehabilitation Commission, the Massachusetts Commission for the Blind, and the Massachusetts Commission for the Deaf and Hard of Hearing. Some youths are *eligible* for adult services through these agencies, but they are not *entitled* to them as they were to services under IDEA. Being eligible is not a guarantee that young adults will receive any of the services that they or their families request. The level of service provision depends on many factors, especially funding. The youths with intellectual disabilities who participated in this study all were eligible for services but had been told to expect a delay in services due to funding issues—the breadth and duration of this gap in service delivery was unknown.

Youths whose disabilities do not fit neatly into the disability silos created by the condition-focused state agencies may also experience a gap, with nowhere to go once they reach adulthood. In Massachusetts, youths who are blind can go to the Massachusetts Commission for the Blind for services; those who have intellectual disabilities can go to the Department of Developmental Services; and those who are deaf or hard of hearing can go to Massachusetts Commission for the Deaf and Hard of Hearing. Parents of youths with learning disabilities or Asperger syndrome could not figure out where to go for disability services and supports when their children left high school. Several parents whose children had Asperger syndrome combined with a mental health condition had reached out to multiple state agencies to no avail. Their children were hot potatoes—no one wanted to take responsibility for them. Lee complained that her son Derek "is a client of DMH [the Department of Mental Health], and they're useless. They have no funding. They fight you on everything. His social worker says, 'Go to Mass Rehab.' And I had to inform her that Mass Rehab doesn't kick in until they're eighteen. His own social worker didn't know that. She goes, 'Oh, I didn't know that.' . . . And DOE [the Department of Education] says, 'Why don't you go to DDS?' And DDS says, 'Why don't you go'—they all just keep passing the buck, and the kid gets nothing." Derek had a dual diagnosis of Asperger syndrome and a mental health condition. The mental health condition made him eligible for DMH-funded services as an adolescent. But when Derek's high school sent a referral for adult services to DMH, DMH rejected it, saying that his primary diagnosis was Asperger syndrome and therefore he would not be eligible for adult services once he left high school. Bob and Rose, whose son Kaiser also had a dual diagnosis of Asperger syndrome and a mental health condition, had similar complaints. They didn't understand why they kept getting passed back and forth from agency to agency and thought that it was unfair that youths with some disabilities such as intellectual disabilities had services while youths like their son did not. Bob said that he "can't see why they can't do it with DMH and DDS, and have one separate agency so that everybody gets equal amounts of funding. Because these kids are getting nothing—*nothing*. And parents are spending thousands of dollars for lawyers. I mean, if we go to a hearing with DMH, we have to get an attorney. And all we're looking for is his record to be corrected and reflect the proper diagnosis [of his mental health condition]." Leslie, whose son Damien also had Asperger syndrome, explained that "it's hit or miss. You've got to just start talking to anybody and everybody, but having said that, there aren't a lot of people that want to listen. It's not their problem. They don't have to deal with it." She hadn't had any luck finding adult services for Kaiser and didn't think that he would have any supports or services after high school.

The organization of disability services is problematic here. The prevalence of youths with Asperger syndrome has increased tremendously over the past few decades, but they do not fit neatly into any of the state agencies that are organized around disabilities that have been recognized and addressed in disability policy since the nineteenth century: blindness, deafness, and intellectual disability. There was an autism division in DDS that did provide some services to children, but youths became ineligible once they reached adulthood. Jeffrey, who son Trevor had autism, said he guessed "the autism division for the government is very small and the budget is very small, which is kind of intriguing where it's 1 out of every 150 kids are now diagnosed with that. Why wouldn't it grow bigger and become more of the budget? Trevor's age isn't going to really get anything out of that. It'll be the next generation of kids because it's more prevalent and services will be more available, I guess. But a lot of parents are upset because at that age when the kids become adults they're thrown to the wind." Some youths might be eligible for services through the Massachusetts Rehabilitation Commission (MRC), which serves people with a wider range of disabilities, but only one set of parents of youths with Asperger syndrome had ever heard of it, and they had unsuccessfully sought services in advance of their son's eighteenth birthday. MRC is trying to address the needs of youths who do not fit into any of the existing adult services silos through an interagency committee that meets periodically. This committee discussed individuals who had disabilities but didn't quite meet the eligibility criteria for any of the state disability agencies. Maya, a professional who knew of this committee, explained that "basically, like, if you send—if a school sends out a 688 [referral for adult state services], one agency might say, 'Oh, this person is not eligible.' So then they get sent to DDS. 'Oh, this person is not eligible.' They send it to DMH. 'This person doesn't fit.' So you're not quite eligible for any particular state agency." At the committee meetings, she said, "they'll throw a file on the table and they'll say, 'Okay, well, maybe MRC will take the voc[ational] piece, and then DDS and/or DMH will provide residential support.' So basically, this person who doesn't fit anywhere but needs services, they get broken up." This committee work helps to eliminate the disability silo problem for some individuals and could perhaps be used to address the needs of youths with Asperger syndrome and dual diagnoses who are coming of age.

There are several other ways to strengthen the links between schools and adult disability agencies. Two ideas have been bandied about recently: using transition specialists, and involving Independent Living Centers (ILCs) more in transition planning and preparation. ILCs could play a much more important role in providing transition services.[9] In fact, this would mean having ILCs return to their roots—the independent living movement was born out of young adults' efforts to transition to independent living. Yet only three of the youths and two of the parents in this study were aware that ILCs existed. The Massachusetts Rehabilitation Commission has a current initiative to become more involved in transition, the Transition to Adulthood Program (TAP). In this program, MRC is contracting with ILCs to provide "early intervention programs" for students with disabilities.[10] TAP primarily serves youths who are transitioning from the Massachusetts Hospital School, which provides rehabilitative care for children and young adults with physical disabilities, but other students can qualify for services if they are between the ages of fourteen and twenty-two, have a severe disability, want to learn independent living and advocacy skills, and are not eligible for services from other state disability agencies (such as the Department of Developmental Services or the Massachusetts Commission for the Blind). Unfortunately, information about this program has not seeped into the information networks which youths and parents are using, mostly schools, parent resource organizations, and other parents. Staff in ILCs across the state are trying to span that gap in awareness by developing relationships with staff in high schools in the areas they serve and by seeking out parents and youths through Special Education Parent Advisory Councils (SEPACs).

The second specific practical suggestion that professionals offered to reduce the gaps between high school and adult disability policies and services was to put transition specialists into place. These transition specialists would understand both the high school systems and the adult systems, and could broker resources and information for youths and parents from both sides of the transition. Norma, a professional who had spent a lot of time and effort on transition issues, thinks "the transition specialist is a critical component. We all come to that. Every initiative that I've sat on, the final thing was the transition specialist. . . . They *will* walk on both sides of the fence. They are going to be in schools, understanding that system, but they also have to have that broad knowledge of adult systems and what those possibilities are. I think only then will you have someone in the school, vested, having that knowledge, having the ability to raise people's expectations by helping them understand systems and the next step."

In Norma's view, transition specialists should be in the schools, but some other professionals felt that they would be equally effective if they were located in adult disability agencies. Ivan in particular felt that we expect too much from schools already. Any additional supports should come from the adult side, in his view. Some states have already put this transition specialist approach into place. Michigan, for example, has transition specialists located in ILCs. In Pennsylvania, there is an Interagency Transition Community of Practice, with transition specialists located in a range of settings. No matter which side of the transition they sit on as their primary location, transition specialists would be human bridges between high school and adult services.

This Generation

Youths with disabilities who are coming of age now have grown up under new rules that promote childhood and youth development in community-based contexts. These new rules open up greater opportunities but also influence individuals' perceptions of what is possible in their lives. The youths who shared their experiences here have high expectations for themselves. Adam, a professional who had a disability, explained that these youths are "normal. They have the same fears; they have the same dreams. Some of them have the same goals and have barriers within their community—some of them more so because of their disability. But these kids are driven. They want to live as productive members of their community. They want to go to school, they want to get jobs, and they don't want to live at home. Even the ones that have good relationships with their parents at home, they want to be on their own . . . they just want to try it."

Youths with intellectual disabilities wanted to work, in a fairly wide range of occupations. Chico, Kayla, and Jessica wanted to do culinary work. William wanted to perform music and clean kitchens. Laura and Mary both wanted to take care of children. Sean wanted to continue working at Target, and Donnie wanted to continue working at Marshalls after finishing school. Many youths with intellectual disabilities aspired to have families of their own someday. Mary wanted to get married, just like her sister. Alan and Cody both wanted to get married too, and both said that they wanted to have two children.

Most youths with hidden, physical, or sensory disabilities wanted to go to college. The few who did not plan to attend college had career plans. Damien wanted to become an auto mechanic and planned to study at a local technical institute after high school. Thomas wanted to become a professional wrestler. If that didn't work out, he planned to join the military, feeling that it would make him more disciplined. The students who aspired to go to college had a variety of interests. Anna was studying to be a veterinary technician. Katherine wanted to be a writer. Emily also wanted to be a writer and hoped to join the Peace Corps after college to "discover some interesting place to settle down." Kevin wanted to eventually pursue his doctorate in the sciences, recognizing that "if I have a bachelor's, I'll just be a lab assistant, and with a master's I'm only going to get to a management position. But if I want something where I can actually do something, I'm going to need to get my doctorate." These dreams and aspirations have very little in common with each other and are the result of individual interests and life experiences. They are as unique as the young people themselves.

Federal disability policy has trickled down to youths, but we need to increase that flow beyond a trickle, especially for youths whose families have fewer resources. By placing primary responsibility on parents to locate resources, we reify existing social inequalities. Knowledge of these new rules is still spotty and uneven—systems could spread knowledge more evenly. We need to address the missing links, the missing connections, between policy and young lives, so that youths can benefit more fully from today's disability policies.

APPENDIX: RESEARCH METHODS

This study was inspired by the transition experiences of Amy Robison, to whom the book is dedicated. I met Amy when she was in her late teens, when I was a graduate student at Brandeis University. Amy is an outspoken young woman who lectures occasionally to medical students, is a theater buff, and gives enthusiastic hugs. She also has Down syndrome. I got to know Amy better right around the time that I finished my Ph.D. and started work on a postdoc at Brandeis. She was working as an intern at the Lemberg Center on the Brandeis campus, a preschool housed within the university. My daughters, Evelyn and Esther, were attending Lemberg and shared Amy's love of musicals, especially *Joseph and the Amazing Technicolor Dreamcoat*. Our families got to know each other fairly well, as Amy's mother, Dotty, and I were friends and colleagues, Amy helped take care of my girls at the Lemberg Center, and Amy's older sister Christina was Esther and Evelyn's favorite babysitter.

Evelyn, Esther, and I attended Amy's high school graduation party, celebrating with her, her family, and their friends. Amy experienced a few bumps after graduation, including a period at home without employment. Through Amy's experiences, I realized that transition from high school could be difficult for youths with disabilities, even for someone with Amy's level of work experience, positive social nature, and extensive family resources. Both her parents worked in the disability field—they were as connected and knowledgeable as parents could be, with Dotty doing disability research on access to health care and on autism, and Rich working as the executive director of the Federation for Children with Special Needs, a federally funded parent resource center in Massachusetts and one of the key sources of information for parents in the state. If Amy and her parents faced difficulties around transition, what was it like for youths and parents who did not have this extraordinary level of knowledge and expertise? I decided to find out and was extremely fortunate that the William T. Grant Foundation chose to support my project through their Scholars Program, providing five years of funding to conduct this study.

Participants

I set out to find youths and parents who wanted to share their transition stories. Of course, there isn't a list of youths with disabilities who are transitioning from high school. So I created as large a net as possible to find youths and parents who might want to participate. I reached out through public school districts, private schools, parent organizations, listservs, and word of mouth. During my outreach, I received approval by the Institutional Review Boards at Simmons College, the Landmark School, and the Massachusetts Hospital School. As a result of the large net I cast, parents and youths volunteered through a range of sources that included the Asperger's Association of New England, the Massachusetts Arc listserv, the Boston College Campus School, the Boston Center for Independent Living, the Boston Public School Parent Advisory Committee, the *Brookline Tab* (a town newspaper), the Cotting School, Easter Seals, the Landmark School, and the Massachusetts Family Voices listserv. I even rented a table at the annual conference of the Federation for Children with Special Needs, hoping to find parents who weren't so well connected and were there seeking information to help their children.

Even though the parents and youths who volunteered came from diverse sources, they all have one thing in common: I was able to locate them because they were connected in some way to an organization that provided resources to youths and parents. I did attempt to recruit a broader population of transitioning youths through several school districts in the Boston metropolitan area but was not successful in convincing the school districts to give me access to youths and parents. (Snoopy sociologists are not always welcome, and special education is often a political hot potato in local school districts.) Therefore, the accounts included in this book represent those of youths and parents who had deliberately sought out resources, although the level of resources they had found varied widely. My recruitment approach means that this book does not include youths and parents who were completely disconnected from sources of support and information. This is important to keep in mind—this is a relatively privileged group of youth. They were largely middle class and their families had some social capital to help them with transition issues. If what I report here seems less than ideal, it most likely represents better than average experiences. Reaching out to resources is a form of parental advocacy, and the youths included here had parents who had reached out and tried to improve their children's opportunities.

Table A.I describes the youths and parents who did agree to participate. Almost two-thirds of the youths are male, which is in line with national statistics showing that two-thirds of students in special education are male.[1] Half the youths had intellectual disabilities (50 percent), one-third had hidden disabilities (33 percent), which includes youths with learning disabilities and Asperger syndrome, and 17 percent had physical or sensory disabilities. From the beginning, I was interested in exploring and comparing the resources and experiences of these three groups of youths with disabilities because of their differences, facilitating comparisons of how supports, skills, and barriers may vary by type of disability. Youths with intellectual disabilities may find a range of opportunities after high school, from competitive employment to supported employment or sheltered workshops or day programs, depending on the nature of their disabilities and the education and training they receive in high school. As a group, adults with intellectual disabilities are among the most vulnerable individuals in U.S. society. They are much more likely than other adults in the general population to live in poverty (28 percent versus II percent) and to live with relatives (62 percent versus 20 percent) (Larson et al. 2001). In Massachusetts, they are also eligible for supports in adulthood in the form of services from the Department of Developmental Services (DDS).

Youths with hidden disabilities may have the option to pass as not disabled and have the greatest degree of choice out of the three groups about disclosing their disabilities. Yet they do not fit neatly under any of the disability service agencies that provide adult supports or services—they may fall between the cracks of the agencies, which have been organized historically around condition-specific silos. It was typically unclear to youths and parents what, if any, state-level disability services were available

	Number	Percent
TABLE A.1		
Characteristics of Youths and Parents		
Gender of youths		
Male	31	60
Female	21	40
Type of disability of youths		
Intellectual	26	50
Hidden	17	33
Physical or sensory	9	17
Race/ethnicity of youths		
Anglo	43	83
Latino	3	6
African American	4	8
Asian	2	4
Family structure		
Intact two-parent	35	67
Divorced, single mother	10	19
Divorced, stepfather in household	4	8
Other	3	6
Housing status of family		
Owned house	47	90
Rented apartment	5	10
Participants interviewed		
Youth only	3	6
Parent(s) only	8	15
Youth and parent(s)	41	79

for these youths once they left high school, but they would be covered by the Americans with Disabilities Act (ADA) in higher education and employment.

Youths with physical and sensory disabilities usually have visible disabilities apparent to those around them—they rarely have the option of passing as nondisabled. Their disabilities are apparent in all social situations, not just in educational contexts, and they may experience discrimination as a result. Of the three groups, they are by far the most likely to complete high school.[2] All the youths with physical or sensory disabilities were also eligible for services from state disability agencies, namely the Massachusetts Rehabilitation Commission, the Massachusetts Commission for the Deaf and Hard of Hearing, or the Massachusetts Commission for the Blind. And they are covered by the ADA in higher education and employment.

I attempted to recruit and interview equal numbers of youths in each of the three disability groupings but was not successful. Parents of youths with intellectual disabilities were the most organized, which meant that they were the easiest to find. Many of these parents found out about the study on the Massachusetts Arc or Mass Family Voices listservs. There wasn't a place like Massachusetts Arc to find parents of youths with learning disabilities—although the majority of children receiving educational services through the Individuals with Disabilities Education Act (IDEA) have learning disabilities, their parents simply are not as organized as parents of children with intellectual disabilities, making it harder to locate them. Youths with physical and sensory disabilities were also difficult to find because their conditions have low prevalence in the general population. So although it is possible to make some comparisons by type of disability here, there are clearly some limitations created by the small number of youths with sensory and physical disabilities included in this study.

We also see in table A.1 that 83 percent of the youths interviewed were white. I did make extensive efforts to include youths of color, through nonprofit, community-based organizations that were organized specifically around race and culture, but met limited success. I also ran a focus group with immigrant mothers to get their advice about recruiting families—although the group discussion was fabulous as mothers made connections across their cultures, I was not successful in recruiting more participants whose children were eligible for the study. Much of my recruiting difficulty was due to my stringent requirements about age (between two years before transition and one year after transition) and disability status (receiving services under IDEA or Section 504). Unfortunately, my limited success in recruiting youths of color precluded me from being able to say much about the role of race or ethnicity in this book. Whenever possible, I've also drawn on the interviews with professionals to supplement information on the importance of race and ethnicity. I deliberately sought out professionals who worked with youths and families of color, hoping to interview those professionals and some of the youths and families with whom they worked. Although I succeeded in interviewing the professionals, it was hard to get access to youths and families. Sometimes the professionals were protective of "their" youths and families and did not feel comfortable facilitating access, and a few times I got a referral but families were wary of me. (There I was, a stranger, from outside their communities, who wanted to ask a lot of personal questions about their children. Why should they trust me?)

In terms of family structure, most of the youths lived in intact families (67 percent), with the rest living with a divorced single mother (19 percent), their mother plus a stepfather (8 percent), or in situations such as extended family, foster care, or living independently (6 percent). Most of the families owned their own home, with the rest renting, several of whom were living in subsidized housing. I wanted to interview both the youth and his or her parent(s) to get both perspectives. Most of the time (79 percent) I succeeded, but it was not always practical. In three situations, we interviewed the youths only—all were youths who had just transitioned from high school, were at least eighteen years old, and were no longer living with their parents. My attempts to contact their parents and invite them to participate were not successful. In eight instances, I interviewed the parents only and the youths were not interviewed—initially this was a situation that I avoided explicitly because I felt that the youths' voices were primary in telling their transition stories and it was not sufficient to have only parental accounts. But in only one of the eight instances did this description fit the situation—when we showed up at one youth's home, she had changed her mind and did not want to be interviewed, but her mother still wanted to participate so I did that interview. In the other seven instances, I interviewed the parent(s) only because we were not able to interview the youths because of communication difficulties. These youths all had intellectual disabilities plus physical disabilities or autism, which made interviewing impossible. Rather than exclude these youths from the study completely, I did interview their parents to capture at least part of their transition stories—these parental interviews are included mostly in chapter 6, "The End of Entitlement," which focuses on the experiences of youths with intellectual disabilities.

Table A.2 describes the group of professionals who participated in the study, all of whom worked with youths and/or parents on transition issues. Four professionals worked for state disability agencies, and the rest worked for nonprofit organizations that received state and/or federal funds to provide disability-related services and information. In terms of gender, the professionals were 40 percent male and 60 percent female. Most were white (75 percent), with two Asian, one Haitian, and two African American participants. Most of the professionals either had a disability themselves (30 percent) or had a close family member with a disability (35 percent), either a child or a sibling.

TABLE A.2
Characteristics of Professionals Interviewed

	Number	Percent
Work setting		
State disability agency	4	20
Nonprofit organization	16	80
Gender		
Male	8	40
Female	12	60
Race/ethnicity		
Anglo	15	75
Asian	2	10
African American	2	10
Haitian	1	5
Personal disability experience		
Has a disability	6	30
Has a close family member with a disability	7	35
Has no personal disability experience	7	35

Interviews

The youth interviews were conducted when the youths were on the cusp of leaving high school—around age eighteen for youths with physical, sensory, or hidden disabilities (learning disabilities or Asperger's syndrome), and around age twenty-two for youths with intellectual disabilities. Youths had to be deemed disabled under one of two pieces of federal disability legislation to be eligible to participate: they received disability-related services or accommodations in high school under the Individuals with Disabilities Education Act (IDEA) or under Section 504 of the Rehabilitation Act. Three youths received services under Section 504 and the rest received them under IDEA.

All the interviews were conducted in person. Participants chose the place of their interviews, and with rare exceptions, youths and parents chose their homes and professionals chose their offices. This meant that we drove all over the state of Massachusetts, wherever people lived and worked. My research assistant, Lexie Waugh, did almost all the youth interviews—her age (early twenties) and open, curious, friendly nature made her a terrific interviewer in this context. Many times, mothers of sons would tell me that I shouldn't expect the young men to say much to Lexie, but then we'd hear echoes of them chatting and laughing from another part of the house. I did all the parent and professional interviews, and did three of the youth interviews with Lexie in the situations where youths had already moved out of their families' homes and the parents were not interested in participating. In seven families, both the mother and father were interviewed; in the remaining families only the mother was interviewed.

All the interviews were semi-structured. The youths' interviews lasted forty-five minutes to one hour, and focused on their dreams and expectations for the future and how they thought about adulthood, transition planning, and their social networks (focused on who they talk with about their future). Parents' interviews lasted one and one-half to two hours, and parents were asked about their dreams and expectations for their children's futures, transition planning, and their social networks (also focused on who they talk with about their children's future). My interviews with professionals lasted one to one and one-half hours and addressed the work that they do with youths and families around transition issues, broader patterns of experiences they have seen among youths with disabilities who are transitioning from high school, and policy recommendations to improve transition to adulthood among youths with disabilities. Written informed consent was obtained from all adult participants. Youths who were under the age of eighteen or were over the age of eighteen but under their parents' guardianship (as was the case for some youths with intellectual disabilities) completed assent forms that contained the same content as the informed consent forms for the adults, plus their parents or guardians gave consent for their participation.

All but four interviews were recorded digitally and the files were transcribed verbatim. (Notes were taken on the other four interviews, as the respondents did not wish to be recorded.) I reviewed all the transcripts, and they were each coded by two people: I coded every interview (youths, parents, and professionals); Lexie also coded all the youth and parent interviews; and my other research assistant at the time, Sheila Rosselli, also coded all the professional interviews.[3] All names used throughout the book are pseudonyms, which were mostly chosen by the participants themselves. Only when participants refused to choose their own pseudonym did we choose one for them. I did this to give participants the ability to name themselves, which will allow them to find and recognize their own experiences in all the publications that result from this project. I hope they enjoy seeing themselves represented here among the transition stories I have told.

NOTES

CHAPTER 1   A CRISIS SITUATION?

1. All participants' names are pseudonyms.

2. For more on the life course perspective and how it is shaped by social context, see Elder, Modell, and Parke 1993.

3. Recently, scholars have focused on how the timing of attainment of markers of adulthood has shifted over the past few decades, possibly with greater variability in their sequencing and longer times to attainment of the full set of adult markers. For more on this topic, see Furstenberg et al. 2004; Goldsheider et al. 1999; Mortimer and Larson 2002; Shanahan 2000; and Shanahan and Hood 2000.

CHAPTER 2   THE RULES HAVE CHANGED

1. See Schwartzenberg 2005 for parents' stories about local school districts' refusal to educate their children.

2. An electronic image of the original letter is available at http://americanhistory .si.edu/disabilityrights/exhibit_parents1_full4.html.

3. Gerben Dejong (1979) also credits the consumerism, self-help, demedicalization, and deinstitutionalization movements as influencing the independent living movement.

4. See Hahn 1994 on the minority model of disability. Mayerson 1993 provides additional information on Americans with Disabilities Act activism.

5. Fleisher and James 2000, 92, quotes Dart's speech, "The ADA: A Promise to Be Kept," from a manuscript the authors received from Dart on May 28, 1997.

6. When Congress created the ADA, it defined a disabled person generally as an individual with "(A) a physical or mental impairment that substantially limits one or more of the major life activities of such individual; (B) a record of such an impairment; or (C) being regarded as having such impairment." Since its passage in 1990, there has been some backlash against the ADA in the courts, in part in an attempt to reduce the scope of individuals who qualify as disabled under the act. In response to these legal challenges to the ADA, Congress passed and President George W. Bush signed the ADA Amendments Act of 2008.

The amended act "reinstates a broad scope of protection under the ADA," stating that "Congress finds that—(1) in enacting the Americans with Disabilities Act of 1990 (ADA), Congress intended that the Act 'provide a clear and comprehensive national mandate for the elimination of discrimination against individuals with disabilities' and provide broad coverage; (2) in enacting the ADA, Congress recognized that physical and mental disabilities in no way diminish a person's right to fully participate in all aspects of society, but that people with physical or mental disabilities are frequently precluded from doing so because of prejudice, antiquated attitudes, or the failure to remove societal and institutional barriers; (3) while Congress expected that the definition of disability under the ADA would be interpreted consistently with how courts had applied the definition of a handicapped individual under the Rehabilitation Act of 1973, that expectation has not been fulfilled." The amended act goes on to specify Supreme Court decisions that narrowed the scope of the ADA.

CHAPTER 3   PARTICIPATION AND VOICE

1. For the Massachusetts Department of Elementary and Secondary Education regulations regarding transition from special education that were effective at the time my fieldwork was conducted, see www.doe.mass.edu/sped/links/transition.html.

2. Similarly, girls with learning disabilities in a recent study of participation in IEP meetings reported that they found the meetings difficult, with one describing them as "intimidating" and another saying that she felt "humiliated" (Trainor 2007, 39). A study of youths with intellectual disabilities conducted in the United Kingdom found that many students were excluded from discussion during planning meetings and that those with more severe disabilities were more likely to be excluded (Carnaby et al. 2003).

CHAPTER 4   MAKING THEIR OWN MAPS

1. Pierre Bourdieu (1986) coined the term "social capital." This chapter relies on James Coleman's (1988) later description of social capital, which spells out additional dimensions of the concept, particularly for youth development.

2. Annette Lareau stressed "the importance of social structural location in shaping their everyday lives" in her investigation of inequality of childhood (2003, 236). Here, social structural location shapes the range of perceived opportunities.

3. Glen H. Elder Jr. has written extensively about how families are important social contexts for youth, particularly in the transition to adulthood, and about how family members' lives are linked and interdependent (see also Elder 1978, 1995; Elder and Caspi 1990); on family roles more recently, see Arnett 2004; Furstenberg et al. 2004. Families can have important effects on the adaptive development of children; for the effects on young children, see Hauser-Cram et al. 1999.

4. Massachusetts recently changed the name of this agency from the Department of Mental Retardation (DMR) to the Department of Developmental Services (DDS), the designation used here.

5. My thanks to Sheila Rosselli for suggesting this concept.

6. For a list from the Technical Assistance Alliance for Parent Centers of all current parent training and information centers in the United States, see www .taalliance.org/.

7. I am grateful to Sheila Rosselli for coining the concept "valid messengers."

8. I interviewed three youths over the age of eighteen living on their own whose parents did not respond to my request for interviews.

9. Mark Mlawer (1993) critiques this advocacy expectation for parents of children with disabilities in the special education system, pointing out that parents are given the responsibility for advocating for their children, but that they often lack the power to influence the processes through which decisions are made. Power and expertise are largely in the hands of professionals.

10. For multiple examples of how disability may be interpreted through cultural lenses, see Ingstad and Whyte 1995.

11. Although in one study, young adults with disabilities said that their parents' efforts on their behalf were key (Pascall and Hendey 2004, 165), the politics of parenting may support parents or may hold them entirely responsible for their children's welfare.

CHAPTER 5   COLLEGE, RIGHTS, AND GOODNESS OF FIT

1. In 2003–2004, 11.3 percent of undergraduates reported having a disability (NCES 2009), almost double the 1995–1996 figure, when only 6 percent of students reported this (Horn and Berktold 1999). The U.S. Department of Education in 2009 classified students who reported that they had one or more of the following conditions as disabled: "a specific learning disability, a visual handicap, hard of hearing, deafness, a speech disability, an orthopedic handicap, or a health impairment" (NCES 2009, 329).

2. For the remainder of the chapter, I use the term "college" to describe both colleges and universities.

3. In the late 1990s, the U.S. Department of Education reported that 72 percent of all two- and four-year postsecondary institutions reported enrolling students with disabilities, but that there was a large difference between public and private institutions. Although 98 percent of public institutions reported enrolling students with disabilities, only 47 percent of private institutions did so (NCES 2000).

4. The phrase "developmental mismatch" was coined to describe problematic changes that early adolescents sometimes experienced when there was a mismatch between their needs and their social environments (Eccles et al. 1993).

This term seems to apply equally well to the older adolescents and young adults here, who experience developmental mismatches between the demands associated with adult disability rights and their lack of advocacy experience and skills and reluctance to engage with an adult disability identity.

5. For a recent review of the literature documenting the higher risk of bullying experienced by youths with disabilities, see Schoen and Schoen 2010.

CHAPTER 6   THE END OF ENTITLEMENT

1. According to the most recent national data available, 4 percent of all youths with disabilities exited at age twenty, compared with 11 percent with intellectual disabilities and 15 percent with multiple disabilities. At age twenty-one, 3 percent of all youths exited, compared with 9 percent of youths with intellectual disabilities and 18 percent of youths with multiple disabilities (DOE 2006).

2. A 2005 memo from the Office of Special Education Programs of the U.S. Department of Education to all state directors of special education outlines each state's cutoff for special education: http://74.125.47.132/search?q=cache:KIQ-2 Nr2MoUJ:www.ed.gov/policy/speced/guid/idea/letters/2005–1/osep0507funds1 q2005.doc.

3. The findings presented here may not be representative of the experiences of students in states where the age cutoffs are earlier and less generous.

4. This description of the "turning twenty-two" process relies on information provided by the Massachusetts Department of Health and Human services at www.mass.gov/?pageID=eohhs2modulechunk&L=3&L0=Home&L1=Consumer& L2=Disability+Services&sid=Eeohhs2&b=terminalcontent&f=mrc_c_turning22_ guide&csid=Eeohhs2.

5. Several parents mentioned that DDS staff told them there might be delays in services, but that DDS staff never used the term "wait list" to describe the situation.

CHAPTER 7   (IM)PERMANENT MARKERS OF ADULTHOOD

1. Considerable work has focused on identifying exactly what constitutes transition in terms of the markers of adulthood, which typically include leaving school, starting full-time work, leaving the home of origin, getting married, and becoming a parent. Most recently, scholars have focused on how the timing of attainment of markers of adulthood has shifted over the past few decades, possibly with greater variability in their sequencing and longer times to attainment of the full set of adult markers (Furstenberg et al. 2004; Goldscheider et al. 1999; Mortimer and Larson 2002; Shanahan 2000; Shanahan and Hood 2000).

2. In response to these changing patterns, some scholars have suggested that more subjective indicators of adulthood may be increasingly helpful in studying this transition (Scheer and Palkovitz 1994; Shanahan, Porfeli, and Mortimer

2004). There is evidence that the traditional role transitions associated with adulthood have declined as cultural markers (Furstenberg et al. 2003).

3. One exception is a recent book that includes youths with disabilities in a chapter on youths exiting public systems but lumps them with children coming out of juvenile justice and foster care systems in one homogenous and problematic population (Foster and Gifford 2005). Other recent exceptions use data from the National Longitudinal Transition Study of Special Education Students (first and second waves) to examine subgroups of special education students (Blackorby and Wagner 1996; Wagner and Blackorby 1996; Wagner et al. 2005; Wells, Sandefur, and Hogan 2003). This research is nuanced in its analysis of the effects of disability status and different types of disabilities. Scholars are only beginning to examine how disability may affect the life course (e.g., Priestley 2000, 2001).

4. These criteria were also examined by gender, but there were no statistically significant differences at the 0.05 level. At the 0.10 level, males were more likely than females to agree that being committed to a long-term love relationship was necessary for achieving adulthood (20 percent versus 14 percent), and females were more likely to agree that reaching age eighteen was necessary (64 percent versus 36 percent).

5. The thirteen youths not included either were not interviewed directly because their disabilities prevented it due to communication issues (nine), they decided not to be interviewed when we arrived at their home (one), or it became apparent during the interview that this set of questions was too abstract for them (three). The latter three youths all had intellectual disabilities and did not understand the nature of the questions—they hesitated before answering each item and asked multiple times for clarification because the questions did not make sense to them. These youths answered more concrete questions about their lives with little or no difficulty, but the questions about what makes individuals adults were too abstract.

CHAPTER 8   MISSING LINKS

1. For example, in 2010 the *New York Times* published two articles on the transition to adulthood (Belkin 2010; Henig 2010) and a book came out on the topic (Settersten and Ray 2010). The MacArthur Foundation has funded an entire network of researchers looking at transition issues, resulting in multiple books, articles, and fact sheets (www.macfound.org/site/c.lkLXJ8MQKrH/b.1009945/k.33C/Research_Networks__Network_on_Transitions_to_Adulthood.htm).

2. Glaser and Strauss (1971:171).

3. Vocational education and community work experience and transportation are crucial issues, but they were not mentioned by any of the youths in the study, and by only a handful of parents and professionals. (Only the youths who had already transitioned had actually faced transportation issues—parents were rarely aware that transportation would be an issue until it became a problem.)

My recommendations are based on the issues that were most pertinent to the youths, parents, and professionals who participated in the study, where I have the strongest and richest data.

4. In the Youth Transition Demonstrations, youth empowerment is defined as "the acquisition of self-knowledge by youth so that they may direct and advocate for their life choices" (Luecking and Wittenberg 2009, 245).

5. This metaphor of a ladder was developed by Hart (1997, 40–45), based on work by Amstein (1969). Additional refinements are provided in Kirby and Woodhead 2003 and Cornwall 2008. Here, I rely primarily upon Perpetua Kirby and Martin Woodhead's descriptions of this ladder.

6. The entire spectrum of participation is as follows, from top to bottom: "(8) Child-initiated, shared decisions with adults (Children and young people have the ideas, set up the project, and invite adults to join with them in making decisions.); (7) Child-initiated and directed (Children and young people have the initial idea and decide how the project is carried out. Adults are available but do not take charge.); (6) Adult-initiated, shared decisions with children (Adults have the initial idea but children and young people are involved in every step of the planning and implementation. Not only are their views considered, but they are also involved in taking [sic] the decisions.); (5) Consulted and informed (The project is designed and run by adults but children and young people are consulted. They have a full understanding of the process and their opinions are taken seriously.); (4) Assigned but informed (Adults decide on the project and children and young people volunteer for it. Adults respect their views and the children feel fully informed.); (3) Tokenism (Children and young people are asked to give their views, but they have little choice about the subject, or about the way that they express themselves, or no time to formulate their opinions.); (2) Decoration (Children and young people promote a cause, e.g., by singing, dancing, or wearing t-shirts with slogans, but they do not really understand the issue, or play any part in organizing events.); (1) Manipulation (Adults consciously use children's voices to carry their own messages.)" (Kirby and Woodhead 2003, 242).

7. Steven Lukes's analysis of power is helpful here in disentangling the effects of adult authority. Lukes describes three dimensions of power. Although all three dimensions could be used in an analysis of youths' participation in IEP transition meetings, it is the third dimension that helps us understand how adults' actions shape youths' participation so profoundly. "To put the matter sharply, A may exercise power over B by getting him to do what he does not want to do, but he also exercises power over him by influencing, shaping, or determining his very wants. Indeed, is it not the supreme exercise of power to get another or others to have the desires you want them to have—that is, to secure their compliance by controlling their thoughts or desires?" (Lukes 1974, 23). Adults have the power to socialize youths into more passive and more active roles when making decisions about their lives.

8. National Dissemination Center for Children with Disabilities, www.nichcy.org/ EducateChildren/transition_adulthood/Pages/Default.aspx.

9. There have been recent calls for such activity on the part of ILCs; see, e.g., Wehmeyer and Gragoudas 2004.

10. The TAP program is described briefly on the Massachusetts Office of Health and Human Services website, http://www.mass.gov/?pageID=eohhs2terminal&L =6&L0=Home&L1=Consumer&L2=Disability+Services&L3=Disability+ Community+Advocacy&L4=Consumer+Involvement&L5=Massachusetts+ Rehabilitation+Commission+Consumer+Handbook&sid=Eeohhs2&b= terminalcontent&f=mrc_c_handbook_cs_06&csid=Eeohhs2#4.

APPENDIX

1. Approximately two-thirds of children receiving Supplemental Security Income (SSI) benefits are boys, as are two-thirds of students receiving special education services (DOE 2001; Tschantz and Markowitz 2003).

2. Their graduation rate is lower than that for youths with no disabilities (63 percent, compared with 81 percent) but is the highest of all disability groups (Larson et al. 2001).

3. All the codes were entered into ATLAS.ti, a qualitative data management and analysis program. Grounded theory was used to guide the analyses—initial, focused, and coaxial coding were conducted, with ongoing review and consensus development regarding themes identified. For more information on grounded theory, see Glaser and Strauss 1967; Strauss 1987.

REFERENCES

Algozzine, Bob, Diane Browder, Meagan Karvonen, David W. Test, and Wendy M. Wood. 2001. "Effects of Interventions to Promote Self-Determination for Individuals with Disabilities." *Review of Educational Research* 71(2): 219–277.

Amstein, Sherry. 1969. "Eight Rungs on the Ladder of Citizen Participation." *Journal of the American Institute of Planners* 35(4): 216–224.

Aquilino, William S. 1999. "Two Views on One Relationship: Comparing Parents' and Young Adult Children's Reports on the Quality of Intergenerational Relations. *Journal of Marriage and the Family* 61(4): 858–870.

Arnett, Jeffrey J. 1997. "Young People's Conceptions of the Transition to Adulthood." *Youth and Society* 29(1): 3–23.

———. 1998. "Learning to Stand Alone: The Contemporary American Transition to Adulthood in Cultural and Historical Context." *Human Development* 41:295–315.

———. 2000. "Emerging Adulthood: A Theory of Development from the Late Teens through the Early Twenties." *American Psychologist* 55(5): 469–480.

———. 2001. "Conceptions of the Transition to Adulthood: Perspectives from Adolescence to Midlife." *Journal of Adult Development* 8(2): 133–143.

———. 2003. "Conceptions of the Transition to Adulthood among Emerging Adults in American Ethnic Groups." *New Directions for Child and Adolescent Development* 100:63–75.

———. 2004. *Emerging Adulthood: The Winding Road from the Late Teens through the Twenties.* New York: Oxford University Press.

Arnett, Jeffrey J., and Jennifer Tanner, eds. 2006. *Emerging Adults in America: Coming of Age in the 21st Century.* Washington, D.C.: American Psychological Association.

Belkin, Lisa. 2010. "The Slow, Winding Path to Adulthood." *New York Times*, April 28. http://parenting.blogs.nytimes.com/2010/04/28/the-slow-winding-path-to-adulthood/.

Berkowitz, Edward D. 1987. *Disabled Policy: America's Programs for the Handicapped.* New York: Cambridge University Press.

Blackorby, Jose, and Mary Wagner. 1996. "Longitudinal Postschool Outcomes of Youth with Disabilities: Findings from the National Longitudinal Transition Study." *Exceptional Children* 62(5): 399–414.

Boggs, Elizabeth M. 1994. "Benchmarks of Change in the Field of Developmental Disabilities." In *Creating Individual Supports for People with Developmental Disabilities,* ed. Valerie J. Bradley, John W. Ashbaugh, and Bruce C. Blaney, 33–57. Baltimore: Paul H. Brookes.

Bourdieu, Pierre. 1986. "The Forms of Capital." In *Handbook of Theory and Research for the Sociology of Education*, ed. John G. Richardson, 241–258. New York: Greenwood Press.

Carnaby, Steven, Patricia Lewis, Di Martin, John Naylor, and David Stewart. 2003. "Participation in Transition Review Meetings: A Case Study of Young People with Learning Disabilities Leaving a Special School." *British Journal of Special Education* 30(4): 187–193.

Carr, Charlie. N.d. The Independent Living Movement: Its Roots and Origins. www.adrc-tae.org/tiki-download_file.php?fileId=26178.

Carroll, Donna Jean. 1971. "A Toast to the Legislators with Love and Homemade Bread." *Seattle Post-Intelligencer*, September 17.

CDC (Centers for Disease Control and Prevention). 2009. *50th Anniversary of the Polio Vaccine: Timeline*. http://www.cdc.gov/vaccines/events/polio-vacc-50th/timeline.htm.

Charlton, James I. 1998. *Nothing about Us without Us: Disability Oppression and Empowerment*. Berkeley: University of California Press.

CIL (Center for Independent Living). 1982. "Independent Living: The Right to Choose." In *Disabled People as Second-Class Citizens*, ed. Myron G. Eisenberg, Cynthia Griggins, and Richard J. Duval, 247–260. New York: Springer.

Coleman, James. 1988. "Social Capital in the Creation of Human Capital." *American Journal of Sociology* 94: S95–S120.

Cornwall, Andrea. 2008. "Unpacking 'Participation': Models, Meanings, and Practices." *Community Development Journal* 43(3): 269–293.

Dehart, Hazel. 2008. "Deconstructing Barriers: Perceptions of Students Labeled with Learning Disabilities in Higher Education." *Journal of Learning Disabilities* 41(6): 483–497.

Dejong, Gerben. 1979. "Independent Living: From Social Movement to Analytical Paradigm." *Archives of Physical Medicine and Rehabilitation* 60(10): 435–446.

DOE (U.S. Department of Education). 2001. *To Assure a Free Appropriate Public Education to All Children with Disabilities: Twenty-third Annual Report to Congress on the Implementation of the Individuals with Disabilities Education Act*. Washington, D.C.: U.S. Department of Education.

———. 2006. *Twenty-Eighth Annual Report to Congress on the Implementation of the Individuals with Disabilities Education Act, Parts B and C*. Washington, D.C.: U.S. Department of Education.

Dowrick, Peter W., John Anderson, Katharina Heyer, and Joie Acosta. 2005. "Postsecondary Education across the USA: Experiences of Adults with Disabilities." *Journal of Vocational Rehabilitation* 22(1): 41–47.

Dybwad, Gunnar. 1983. "The Achievements of Parent Organizations." In *Parent Professional Partnerships in Developmental Disability Services*, ed. James A. Mulick and Sigfried M. Pueschel, 197–205. Cambridge, Mass.: Ware Press.

Dybwad, Rosemary. 1990. *Perspectives on a Parent Movement: The Revolt of Parents of Children with Intellectual Disabilities*. Cambridge, Mass.: Brookline Books.

Eccles, Jacquelynne S., Carol Midgley, Allan Wigfield, Christy Miller Buchanan, David Reuman, Constance Flanagan, and Douglas MacIver. 1993. "Development during Adolescence: The Impact of Stage-Environment Fit on Young Adolescents' Experiences in Schools and in Families." *American Psychologist* 48(2): 90–101.

Eckes, Suzanne E., and Theresa A. Ochoa. 2005. "Students with Disabilities: Transitioning from High School." *American Secondary Education* 33(3): 6–20.

Elder, Glen H., Jr. 1978. "Family History and the Life Course." In *Transitions: The Family and the Life Course in Historical Perspective*, ed. Tamara K. Hareven, 17–64. New York: Academic Press.

———. 1991. "Lives and Social Change." In *Theoretical Advances in Life Course Research*, ed. Walter R. Heinz, 58–114. Weinham, Germany: Deutscher Studies Verlag.

———. 1995. "The Life Course Paradigm: Social Change and Individual Development." In *Examining Lives in Context: Perspectives on the Ecology of Human Development*, ed. Phyllis Moen, Glen H. Elder Jr., and Karl Lüscher, 101–139. Washington, D.C.: American Psychological Association.

———. 1998. "The Life Course as Developmental Theory." *Child Development* 69(1): 1–12.

Elder, Glen H., Jr., and Avshalom Caspi. 1990. "Studying Lives in a Changing Society: Sociological and Personological Explorations." In *Studying Persons and Lives*, ed. Albert I. Rabin, Robert A. Zucker, Robert A. Emmons, and Susan Frank, 201–247. New York: Springer.

Elder, Glen H., Jr., John Modell, and Ross D. Parke. 1993. *Children in Time and Place: Developmental and Historical Insights*. New York: Cambridge University Press.

Engel, David M. 1993. "Narratives of Authority, Resistance, Disability, and Law." *Law and Society Review* 27(4): 785–826.

Engel, David M., and Frank W. Munger. 2003. *Rights of Inclusion: Law and Identity in the Life Stories of Americans with Disabilities*. Chicago: University of Chicago Press.

Fay, Fred, and Fred Pelka. 2003. "Justin Dart, an Obituary." www.aapd-dc.org/docs/jdanobiltuary.html.

Fenton, Joseph, Andrew Batavia, and Deborah S. Roody. 1993. *Proposed Policy Statement for NIDRR on Constituency-Oriented Research and Dissemination*. Washington, DC: National Institute on Disability and Rehabilitation Research.

Field, Sharon, and Alan Hoffman. 2002. "Lessons Learned from Implementing the *Steps to Self-Determination* Curriculum." *Remedial and Special Education* 23(2): 90–98.

Finger, Anne. 2006. *Elegy for a Disease: A Personal and Cultural History of Polio*. New York: St. Martin's Press.

Fleischer, Doris Zames, and Frieda Zames. 2000. *Disability Rights Movement*. Philadelphia: Temple University Press.

Foster, E. Michael, and Elizabeth J. Gifford. 2005. Developmental and Administrative Transitions for Special Populations: Policies, Outcomes, and Research Challenges. In *On the Frontier of Adulthood: Theory, Research, and Public Policy*, ed. Richard A. Settersten Jr., Frank F. Furstenberg Jr., and Rubén G. Rumbaut, 501–533. Chicago: University of Chicago Press.

Furstenberg, Frank F., Sheela Kennedy, Vonnie C. McCloyd, Rubén G. Rumbaut, and Richard A. Settersten. 2003. *"Between Adolescence and Adulthood: Expectations about the Timing of Adulthood."* Research working paper I. http://www.pop.upenn.edu/transad/.

———. 2004. "Growing Up Is Harder to Do." *Contexts* 3(3): 33–41.

GAO (U.S. General Accounting Office). 2003. *Special Education: Federal Actions Can Assist States in Improving Postsecondary Outcomes for Youth.* Washington, D.C.: General Accounting Office.

Gaventa, John. 1982. *Power and Powerlessness: Quiescence and Rebellion in an Appalachian Valley.* Urbana and Chicago: University of Illinois Press.

Glaser, Barney G., and Anselm L. Strauss. 1967. *The Discovery of Grounded Theory: Strategies for Qualitative Research.* Chicago: Aldine.

———. 1971. *Status Passage.* New York: Aldine.

Goffman, Erving. 1963. *Stigma: Notes on the Management of Spoiled Identity.* New York: Simon and Schuster.

Goldscheider, Frances, Calvin Goldscheider, Patricia St. Clair, and James Hodges. 1999. "Changes in Returning Home in the United States, 1925–1985." *Social Forces* 78(2): 695–728.

Hadley, Wanda M. 2006. "L.D. Students' Access to Higher Education: Self-Advocacy and Support." *Journal of Developmental Education* 30(2): 10–16.

Hahn, Harlan. 1994. "The Minority Group Model of Disability: Implications for Medical Sociology." *Research in Sociology of Health Care* 11:3–24.

Hamilton, Stephen F., and Mary Agnes Hamilton. 2006. "School, Work, and Emerging Adulthood." In *Emerging Adults in America: Coming of Age in the 21st Century,* ed. Jeffrey J. Arnett and Jennifer L. Tanner, 257–277. Washington, D.C.: American Psychological Association.

Hart, Roger A. 1992. *Children's Participation: From Tokenism to Citizenship.* Florence, Italy: UNICEF International Child Development Centre.

———. 1997. *Children's Participation, the Theory and Practice of Involving Young Citizens in Community Development and Environmental Care.* London: Earthscan Publications.

Hartman-Hall, Heather M., and David A. F. Haaga. 2002. "College Students' Willingness to Seek Help for Their Learning Disabilities." *Learning Disability Quarterly* 25(4): 263–274.

Hauser-Cram, Penny, Marjorie Warfield, Marty Krauss, Jack Shonkoff, Carol Upshur, and Aline Sayer. 1999. "Family Influences on Adaptive Behavior in Young with Down Syndrome." *Child Development* 70(4): 979–989.

Henig, Robin Marantz. 2010. "What Is It about 20-Somethings?" *New York Times Magazine,* August 10. http://www.nytimes.com/2010/08/22/magazine/22Adulthood-t.html?pagewanted=all.

Hogan, Dennis P., and Nan Marie Astone. 1986. "The Transition to Adulthood." *Annual Review of Sociology* 12:109–130.

Horn, Laura, and Jennifer Berktold. 1999. *Students with Disabilities in Postsecondary Education: A Profile of Preparation, Participation, and Outcomes.* National Center for Educational Statistics, U.S. Department of Education. NCES 1999–187. Washington D.C.: U.S. Department of Education.

Howe, R. Brian, and Katherine Covell. 2005. *Empowering Children: Children's Rights Education as a Pathway to Citizenship*. Buffalo, N.Y.: University of Toronto Press.

Ingstad, Benedicte, and Susan Reynolds Whyte, eds. 1995. *Disability and Culture*. Berkeley: University of California Press.

Janus, Alexander L. 2009. "Disability and the Transition to Adulthood." *Social Forces* 88(1): 99–120.

Jennings, Louise B., Deborah M. Parra-Medina, DeAnne K. Hilfinger Messias, and Kerry McLoughlin. 2006. "Toward a Critical Social Theory of Youth Empowerment." *Journal of Community Practice* 14(1, 2): 31–55.

Jones, Kathleen W. 2004. "Education for Children with Mental Retardation: Parent Activism, Public Policy, and Family Ideology in the 1950s." In *Mental Retardation in America: A Historical Reader*, ed. Steven Noll and James W. Trent Jr., 322–350. New York: New York University Press.

Kirby, Perpetua, and Martin Woodhead. 2003. "Children's Participation in Society." In *Changing Childhoods: Local and Global*, ed. Heather Montgomery, Rachel Burr, and Martin Woodhead, 233–284. New York: John Wiley and Sons.

Kravitz, Marybeth, and Imy Wax. 2001. *The Princeton Review K&W Guide for Colleges for Students with Learning Disabilities or ADD*. Framingham, Mass.: Princeton Review.

Landsdown, Gerison. 1995. *Taking Part: Children's Participation in Decision Making*. London: Institute for Public Policy Research.

Lareau, Annette. 2000. *Home Advantage: Social Class and Parental Intervention in Elementary Education*. Berkeley: University of California Press.

———. 2003. *Unequal Childhoods: Class, Race, and Family Life*. Berkeley: University of California Press.

Larson, Sheryl, Charlie Lakin, Lynda Anderson, and Nohoon Kwak. 2001. *MR/DD Data Brief: Demographic Characteristics of Persons with MR/DD Living in Their Own Homes or with Family Members: NHIS-D Analysis*. Minneapolis: Institute on Community Integration, University of Minnesota.

Leiter, Valerie. 2004a. "Dilemmas in Sharing Care: Maternal Provision of Professionally-Driven Therapy for Children with Disabilities." *Social Science and Medicine* 58(4): 837–849.

———. 2004b. "Parental Activism and Professional Dominance, and Early Childhood Disability." *Disability Studies Quarterly*. www.dsq-sds.org.

Leiter, Valerie, Marty W. Krauss, Betsy Anderson, and Nora Wells. 2004. "The Consequences of Caring: Maternal Impacts of Having a Child with Special Needs." *Journal of Family Issues* 25(3): 379–403.

Luecking, Richard G., and David Wittenberg. 2009. "Providing Supports to Youth with Disabilities Transitioning to Adulthood: Case Descriptions from the Youth Transition Demonstration." *Journal of Vocational Rehabilitation* 30:241–251.

Lukes, Steven. 1974. *Power: A Radical View*. New York: Macmillan.

Mackie, Romaine. 1969. *Special Education in the U.S.: Statistics, 1948–1966*. New York: Teachers College Press.

Mangrum, Charles T., II, and Stephen S. Strichart. 1997. *Peterson's Colleges with Programs for Students with Learning Disabilities or Attention Deficit Disorders*. 5th ed. Lawrenceville, N.J.: Peterson's.

Marini, Margaret Mooney. 1984. "The Order of Events in the Transition to Adult-hood." *Sociology of Education* 57(April): 63–84.

Martin, Edwin W., Reed Martin, and Donna L. Terman. 1996. "The Legislative and Litigation History of Special Education." *Future of Children* 6(1): 25–39.

MDMR (Massachusetts Department of Mental Retardation). 2002. *Annual Report: July 1, 2001–June 30 2002.* www.mass.gov/Eeohhs2/docs/dmr/annualrpt_fy02.rtf.

———. 2008. *The Road Forward: A DMR Guide to Transition Planning.* Boston: Massachusetts Department of Mental Retardation.

Mayerson, Arlene. 1993. "The History of the ADA: A Movement Perspective." In *Implementing the Americans with Disabilities Act: Rights and Responsibilities of All Americans,* ed. Lawrence O. Gostin and Henry A. Beyer, 17–24. Baltimore: Paul H. Brookes.

Meyer, Madonna Harrington, ed. 2000. *Care Work: Gender, Labor, and the Welfare State.* New York: Routledge.

Mlawer, Mark A. 1993. "Who Should Fight? Parents and the Advocacy Expectation." *Journal of Disability Policy Studies* 4(1): 105–116.

Modell, John. 1989. *Into One's Own: From Youth to Adulthood in the United States, 1920–1975.* Berkeley: University of California Press.

Mortimer, Jeylan T., and Reed W. Larson. 2002. "Macrostructural Trends and the Reshaping of Adolescence." In *The Changing Adolescent Experience: Societal Trends and the Transition to Adulthood,* ed. Jeylan T. Mortimer and Reed W. Larson, 1–17. New York: Cambridge University Press.

NCD (National Council on Disability and Social Security Administration). 2000. *Transition and Post-School Outcomes for Youth with Disabilities: Closing the Gaps to Post-Secondary Education and Employment.* Washington, D.C.: Social Security Administration.

NCES (National Center for Educational Statistics, U.S. Department of Education). 2000. *Postsecondary Students with Disabilities: Enrollment, Services, and Persistence. Stats in Brief.* http://nces.ed.gov/pubs2000/2000092.pdf.

———. 2008. *Digest of Education Statistics, 2007.* http://nces.ed.gov/programs/digest/d07/tables/dt07_191.asp.

———. 2009. *Digest of Education Statistics, 2008.* http://nces.ed.gov/pubs2009/2009020.pdf.

NCES/OERI (National Center for Educational Statistics, U.S. Department of Education, Office of Educational Research and Improvement. 2000. *Postsecondary Students with Disabilities: Enrollment, Services, and Persistence.* http://nces.ed.gov/pubs2000/2000092.pdf.

NCSER (National Center for Special Education Research, U.S. Department of Education). 2009. *The Post-High School Outcomes of Youth with Disabilities up to 4 Years after High School.* Washington, D.C.: U.S. Department of Education. http://ies.ed.gov/ncser/pubs/20093017/index.asp.

Nelson, Larry J. 2003. "Rites of Passage in Emerging Adulthood: Perspectives of Young Mormons." *New Directions for Child and Adolescent Development* 100: 33–49.

Nelson, Larry J., and Carolyn McNamara Barry. 2005. "Distinguishing Features of Emerging Childhood: The Role of Self-Classification as an Adult." *Journal of Adolescent Research* 20(2): 242–262.

Nelson, Larry J., Laura M. Padilla-Walker, Jason S. Carroll, Carolyn McNamara Barry, Stephanie D. Madsen, and Sarah Badger. 2007. "'If You Want Me to Treat You Like an Adult, Start Acting Like One!': Comparing the Criteria That Emerging Adults and Their Parents Have for Adulthood." *Journal of Family Psychology* 21(4): 665–674.

Osgood, Robert L. 2005. *The History of Inclusion in the United States*. Washington, D.C.: Gallaudet University Press.

———. 2008. *The History of Special Education: A Struggle for Equality in American Public Schools*. Westport, Conn.: Praeger.

Pascall, Gillian, and Nicola Hendey. 2004. "Disability and Transition to Adulthood: The Politics of Parenting." *Critical Social Policy* 24(2): 165–186.

PCMR (President's Committee on Mental Retardation). 1977. *Mental Retardation Past and Present*. Washington, D.C.: President's Committee on Mental Retardation.

Pelka, Fred. 1997. *ABC-CLIO Companion to the Disability Rights Movement*. Santa Barbara, Calif.: ABC-CLIO.

Powers, Laurie E., George H. S. Singer, and Bonnie Todis. 1996. "Reflections on Competence: Perspectives of Successful Adults." In *On the Road to Autonomy: Promoting Self-Competence in Children and Youth with Disabilities*, ed. Laurie E. Powers, George H. S. Singer, and Jo-Ann Sowers, 69–92. Baltimore: Paul H. Brookes.

Price, Lynda A., Paul J. Gerber, and Robert Mulligan. 2007. "Adults with Learning Disabilities and the Underutilization of the Americans with Disabilities Act." *Remedial and Special Education* 28(6): 340–344.

Priestley, Mark. 2000. "Adults Only: Disability, Social Policy, and the Life Course." *Journal of Social Policy* 29(3): 421–439.

———, ed. 2001. *Disability and the Life Course: Global Perspectives*. Cambridge: Cambridge University Press.

Roberts, Ed. 1977. Celebrating a Disability Rights Milestone: Ed Roberts' 504 Victory Speech. http://www.wid.org/news/celebrating-a-disability-rights-milestone-ed-roberts-504-victory-speech.

Sahlen, Cheryl A. Hurtubis, and Jean P. Lehmann. 2006. "Requesting Accommodations in Higher Education." *Teaching Exceptional Children* 38(3): 29–34.

Scheer, Scott D., and Robin Palkovitz. 1994. "Adolescent-to-Adult Transitions: Social Status and Cognitive Factors." *Sociological Studies of Children* 6:125–140.

Scheerenberger, R. C. 1987. *A History of Mental Retardation: A Quarter Century of Promise*. Baltimore: Paul H. Brookes.

Schoen, Sharon, and Alexis Schoen. 2010. "Bullying and Harassment in the United States." *Clearing House* 83(2): 68–72.

Schwartzenberg, Susan. 2005. *Becoming Citizens: Family Life and the Politics of Disability*. Seattle: University of Washington Press.

Scotch, Richard K. 1984. *From Good Will to Civil Rights: Transforming Federal Disability Policy*. Philadelphia: Temple University Press.

Scott, Sally S. 1991. "A Change in Legal Status: An Overlooked Dimension in the Transition to Higher Education." *Journal of Learning Disabilities* 24(8): 459–466.

Segal, Robert M. 1970. *Mental Retardation and Social Action: A Study of the Associations for Retarded Citizens as a Force for Social Change*. Springfield, Ill.: Charles C. Thomas.

Settersten, Richard, and Barbara E. Ray. 2010. *Not Quite Adults: Why 20-Somethings Are Choosing a Slower Path to Adulthood, and Why It's Good for Everyone.* New York: Bantam.

Shanahan, Michael J. 2000. "Pathways to Adulthood in Changing Societies: Variability and Mechanisms in Life Course Perspective." *Annual Review of Sociology* 26:667–692.

Shanahan, Michael J., and Kathryn E. Hood. 2000. "Adolescents in Changing Social Structures: Bounded Agency in Life Course Research." In *Negotiating Adolescence in Times of Social Change,* ed. Lisa J. Crockett and Rainer K. Silbereisen, 123–134. New York: Cambridge University Press.

Shanahan, Michael, Erik Porfeli, and Jeylan Mortimer. 2004. *What Marks Adulthood— Subjective Identity or Demographic Markers?* Network on Transitions to Adulthood Policy Brief. MacArthur Foundation Research Network on Transitions to Adulthood and Public Policy. http://www.transad.pop.upenn.edu/news/chap%207-formatted.pdf.

Shapiro, Joseph. 1994. *No Pity: People with Disabilities Forging a New Civil Rights Movement.* New York: Three Rivers Press.

Shriver, Eunice Kennedy. 2004. "Hope for Retarded Children." In *Mental Retardation in America: A Historical Reader,* ed. Steven Noll and James W. Trent Jr., 303–307. New York: New York University Press.

Silver, Julie, and Daniel J. Wilson. 2007. *Polio Voices: An Oral History from the American Polio Epidemics and Worldwide Eradication Efforts.* Santa Barbara, Calif.: Praeger.

Sitlington, Patricia L., and Erin M. Payne. 2004. "Information Needed by Postsecondary Education: Can We Provide It as Part of the Transition Assessment Process?" *Learning Disabilities: A Contemporary Journal* 2(2): 1–14.

Strauss, Anselm. 1987. *Qualitative Analysis for Social Scientists.* New York: Cambridge University Press.

Switzer, Jacqueline Vaughn. 2003. *Disabled Rights: American Disability Policy and the Fight for Equality.* Washington, D.C.: Georgetown University Press.

Tanner, Jennifer L. 2006. "Recentering during Emerging Adulthood: A Critical Turning Point in Life Span Human Development." In *Emerging Adults in America: Coming of Age in the 21st Century,* ed. Jeffrey J. Arnett and Jennifer L. Tanner, 21–55. Washington, D.C.: American Psychological Association.

Test, David W., Christine Mason, Carolyn Hughes, Moira Konrad, Melia Neale, and Wendy M. Wood. 2004. "Student Involvement in Individualized Education Program Meetings." *Exceptional Children* 70(4): 391–412.

Tisdall, E. Kay M. 1994. "Why Not Consider Citizenship? A Critique of Post-School Transitional Models for Young Disabled People." *Disability and Society* 9(1): 3–17.

Trainor, Audrey A. 2007. "Perceptions of Adolescent Girls with LD Regarding Self-Determination and Postsecondary Transition Planning." *Learning Disability Quarterly* 30 (Winter): 31–45.

Traustadóttir, Rannveig. 2000. "Disability Reform and Women's Caring Work." In *CareWork: Gender, Labor, and the Welfare State,* ed. Madonna Harrington Meyer, 249–269. New York: Routledge.

Trent, James. 1994. *Inventing the Feeble Mind: A History of Mental Retardation in the United States*. Berkeley: University of California Press.

Tschantz, Jennifer, and Joy Markowitz. 2003. *Gender and Special Education: Current State Data Collection. Quick Turn Around*. Alexandria, Va.: National Association of State Directors of Special Education.

Wagner, Mary M., and Jose Blackorby. 1996. "Transition from High School to Work or College: How Special Education Students Fare." *Future of Children* 6(1): 103–120.

Wagner, Mary, Lynn Newman, and Renée Cameto. 2004. *Changes over Time in the Secondary School Experiences of Students with Disabilities: A Report of Findings from the National Longitudinal Transition Study (NLTS) and the National Longitudinal Transition Study-2 (NLTS2)*. Menlo Park, Calif.: SRI International. www.nlts2.org/reports/changestime_report.html.

Wagner, Mary, Lynn Newman, Renée Cameto, and Phyllis Levine. 2005. *Changes over Time in the Early Postschool Outcomes of Youth with Disabilities: A Report of Findings from the National Longitudinal Transition Study (NLTS) and the National Longitudinal Transition Study-2 (NLTS2)*. Menlo Park, Calif.: SRI International. www.nlts2.org/reports/2005_06/nlts2_report_2005_06_ complete.pdf.

Wehmeyer, Michael L., and Stelios Gragoudas. 2004. "Centers for Independent Living and Transition-Age Youth: Empowerment and Self-Determination." *Journal of Vocational Rehabilitation* 20:53–58.

Wehmeyer, Michael L., and Michelle Schwartz. 1997. Self-Determination and Positive Adult Outcomes: A Follow-up Study of Youth with Mental Retardation or Learning Disabilities." *Exceptional Children* 63(2): 245–255.

Wells, Thomas, Gary D. Sandefur, and Dennis P. Hogan. 2003. "What Happens after the High School Years among Young Persons with Disabilities?" *Social Forces* 82(2): 803–832.

West, Michael, John Kregel, Elizabeth E. Getzel, Ming Zhu, Shyla M. Ipsen, and E. Davis Martin. 1993. "Beyond Section 504: Satisfaction and Empowerment of Students with Disabilities in Higher Education." *Exceptional Children* 59(5): 456–467.

Wickham-Searl, Parnel. 1994. "Mothers of Children with Disabilities and the Construction of Expertise." *Research in Sociology of Health Care* 11:175–187.

Wong, Naima T., Marc Z. Zimmerman, and Edith A. Parker. 2010. "A Typology of Youth Participation and Empowerment for Child and Adolescent Health Promotion." *American Journal of Community Psychology* 46:100–114.

Young, Jonathan M. 1997. *Equality of Opportunity: The Making of the Americans with Disabilities Act*. Washington, D.C.: National Council on Disability.

Zimmerman, Marc A., and Seth Warschausky. 1998. "Empowerment Theory for Rehabilitation Research: Conceptual and Methodological Issues." *Rehabilitation Psychology* 43(1): 3–16.

Zola, Irving K. 1983. "Toward Independent Living: Goals and Dilemmas." In *Independent Living for Physically Disabled Persons*, ed. Nancy M. Crewe and Irving K. Zola, 344–356. San Francisco: Jossey-Bass.

INDEX

ABOUT THE AUTHOR

VALERIE LEITER is an associate professor of sociology at Simmons College. Her work focuses on children and youth with disabilities, their families, and public policies that address their lives. She is the coeditor of *Health and Health Care as Social Problems* and of the ninth edition of *The Sociology of Health & Illness: Critical Perspectives* (both with Peter Conrad).

CPSIA information can be obtained at www.ICGtesting.com
Printed in the USA
BVOW072332310112

281770BV00001B/1/P